Still Not Enough

Minority Millennials in the Workforce

Still Not Enough

Minority Millennials in the Workforce

Janelle A. Jordan, DBA

Fresh Ink Group
Guntersville

Still Not Enough:
Minority Millennials in the Workforce

Fresh Ink Group
An Imprint of:
The Fresh Ink Group, LLC
1021 Blount Avenue #931
Guntersville, AL 35976
Email: info@FreshInkGroup.com
FreshInkGroup.com

Edition 1.0   2022

Cover design by Stephen Geez / FIG
Cover Photo by Jarrett Polite
Book design by Amit Dey / FIG
Edited by Maryam Nawaz
Associate publisher Lauren A. Smith / FIG

Cataloging-in-Publication Recommendations:
BIO003000 / BIOGRAPHY & AUTOBIOGRAPHY / Business
BIO026000 / BIOGRAPHY & AUTOBIOGRAPHY / Personal Memoirs
BUS097000 / BUSINESS & ECONOMICS / Workplace Culture

Library of Congress Control Number: 2022909298

ISBN-13: 978-1-947893-49-8 Papercover
ISBN-13: 978-1-947893-50-4 Hardcover
ISBN-13: 978-1-947893-51-1 Ebooks

Contents

This book is dedicated to every person in a position of influence who sought to impose their perspective to keep minority Millennials from attaining and keeping well-earned roles. Your decisions continue to fuel the fire and propel the momentum to do more from both minority Millennials and our advocates.

Acknowledgments

My utmost appreciation, first and foremost, goes to God. He has given me clarity and vision beyond what I could comprehend at the time. It is His grace and mercy that has brought me throughout my journey. I extend my thanks to my family and those friends who have become family.

Thanks to my mentors and sounding boards who challenge me with alternative perspectives, allow me to vent, and then tell me to pull it together. It is always a two-way dialogue with my mentees, who have taught me more than you realize. I am only as strong as these people who have kept me balanced.

While I have not listed everyone specifically for fear of inadvertently leaving someone who has made an impact out. I thank you for what you have poured into me, and I thank you for your love.

"Do not go where the path may lead, go instead where there is no path and leave a trail."

—Ralph Waldo Emerson

Preface

In today's workforce, declarations exist on behalf of organizations for equality and diversity amongst their tiers. This is predicated on the years of unequal pay, affirmative action, and the need to have those in managerial roles reflect that of consumers. This need for diversification is not only premised on the physical makeup of employees, but on the miscellany of thought to represent societal norms.

Theoretically, this is what most organizations have stated their goal is and what they plan to achieve. Practically, this is not what has been experienced by those minorities who hold true to the statements made to stakeholders and consumers alike to show progressive action. While this is not representative of the sentiments of each person in the dominant race and gender, it is still embodied by those in managerial ranks deciding to exemplify what organizations are perceived to represent.

Likewise, the views expressed in this book do not represent the views of every minority Millennial in the workforce. However, it tells a repeated trend of the need to be better than our counterparts in the workforce, which is seemingly still not enough. As they dare not be labeled as leaders, managers are blinded by the unconscious biases of their upbringings and their inability to diversify their perspectives based on what is traditionally perceived to exist and what is exuded in the workforce.

This book seeks to outline the background and experiences of the minority Millennials while cleaning the lenses of those blinded by their own innate inclinations. It also teaches references and guides leadership in being more than enough and setting your own path. It reminds the importance of communicating and seeing other sides of the spectrum in navigating today's transitioning workforce.

Chapter 1
Humble Beginnings

As we start this book, we will delve into my humble beginnings. For some, it may beg to question the need to expound upon one's upbringings in another book that dispels existing disparities; this context builds upon the narrative on what has contributed to my cultural influences and viewpoint on how I view the world.

My grandparents, who helped in solidifying my intrinsic motivation and passion to succeed, are the foundation of my parents and of which my siblings and I encompass. I did not know my paternal grandfather because of his early passing but spent a lot of my time growing up with my paternal grandmother, Andrew Louise Jordan. She was a solid yet feisty African American woman who loved everyone she encountered. Although she only had a tenth-grade education, she was always full of wisdom and 'isms' that we still use today. She always got things done, which could be attributed to her hustler ambition. This allowed her to dream big and show it through her fashionable attire. When people speak of her, they consistently mention her being a sharp dresser and a wonderful cook.

Once back in Orangeburg, South Carolina, from the Big Apple, my grandmother began working at South Carolina State College, which is now South Carolina State University. She ran the cafeteria, fed many both on- and off-campus, and became a mother figure to several football players with whom she maintained a relationship well after her retirement. My grandmother was also an avid activist and supporter in the Sunnyside Community of Orangeburg. This is the neighborhood my family grew up in and was known as one of the hoods of Orangeburg, commonly referenced as 'The Burg'. She joined sides with local law enforcement to work on protecting the neighborhood but would also post bail if needed. She was a mother to many, a cook, 'The Sheriff', 'The Bail Bondsmen', but more affectionately known by many as 'Mother J'. My father's side of the family is significant, considering the number of aunts, uncles, and cousins I have, which explains my love for family.

My maternal grandparents were divorced as far back as I can recall on my mother's side. To their union, two girls were born, with my mother being the oldest of the two. The maternal side of my family is small but rooted in diverse backgrounds. My grandfather was of West Indian descent and resided in Brooklyn, New York. He remarried and made his living as a merchant. As far back as I remember, whenever we would visit or talk on the phone, he would always talk about my future in education. He always told me computers were the way of the future, and I needed to learn them and focus on that as a career.

My maternal grandmother was of African American and Sioux Indian descent. She lived in Bronx, New York, and worked as an assistant and teacher's aide at Immaculate Conception. We would speak to her often, and it was always so exciting to receive and send letters in the mail to her. She was big on the value of writing notes while also focusing on penmanship and being able to read and write in cursive. I also can't forget to wrap a package with mounds of tape to ensure no one tampered with what was inside. My grandmother would come to visit us much more than my grandfather, and we would go spend some summers in the Bronx with her. She, too, was quite the cook and earned the love and respect of those in her housing project. My grandmother was reminiscent of Pearl from the television show 227. Pearl used to look out of the window and talk to the neighbors on the show. Well, that was my grandmother. She would often look out of her apartment window and signal she saw us upon our arrival. My grandmother was a devout Catholic with a loving spirit. Not to mention a diehard New York Yankees fan and, believe it or not, a Dallas Cowboys fan. Being a Cowboys fan was a typical love she and my father shared.

I was born in June 1983 at Presbyterian Children's Hospital in Manhattan, New York, yet home for us was Bronx, New York. I was the youngest of three siblings, Anjelica and Janese. There was no set name for me as I entered this world, but with the help of a magazine, my parents could name me. Like in most households, I was given a nickname, namely 'Miss Piggy' regarding the character of the Muppet Babies. This was because of my chubby physique and pink complexion at birth. I was the final chapter in my parent's book of kids as happiness, excitement, and some surprises were brought on by my birth. It was never in the plan for my parents to have a third child. Even more of a surprise as my mother almost delivered me to the toilet. She thought she was experiencing stomach pangs from the food she ate the night before. One person, Janese, was not exactly thrilled as she now assumed the role of the middle child. For Anjelica, I was her baby.

Looking back on how my parents first met, you can say love works in mysterious ways. My father was a 'southern boy' from Orangeburg, South Carolina. Fresh out of high school, my father moved to the busy city of the Bronx, New York, trying to grasp the feel of life. In other words, he was eager to show he was grown, and what better place than where my grandmother also had spent her time with other members of the family. Upon initially arriving, my father worked at a furniture store in Manhattan and later at a Bankers Trust Branch, also located in Manhattan.

My mother was a native of the Bronx and had recently given birth to her first baby girl during her first semester of college. After accepting the responsibility of being a single mother, my mother dropped out of school and began looking for employment. On her first day out looking for a job, she also found a job at Bankers Trust as a clerk.

My mother started her job the following week and began meeting new people. In her attempt to meet new people, her Assistant Supervisor invited her and another new female employee to join a group of people from the Collections Department to go bowling or have a good time after work. Both my mother and the other young lady agreed to go; however, the other female employee did not show up when the time came. The Assistant Supervisor intended to do some matchmaking at the time; thus, he brought his friend Andrew, my father, along for the outing. It was not initially arranged for my parents to be matched, but for my father to meet the other new female employee. Because of her absence, my mother and father were then introduced. They talked and laughed until it was time for my mother to leave. They then exchanged phone numbers and soon started dating. Later, they were engaged and finally married. As all marriages have ups and downs, my parents resolved to go their separate ways and divorced after over 20 years of marriage.

From my parents' union was the formation of 'Those Jordan Girls'. My eldest sister, Anjelica, tended to me as her own. With nine years between us, she was often left to look out and take care of Janese and me. While she does not share the same biological father as Janese and me, my father embraced her as his own when he began dating my mother. Her path is diverse in being born to a Puerto Rican father and African American mother. Anjelica attended Catholic schools in the Bronx and later in our move to Orangeburg, specifically Immaculate Conception and Holy Trinity. She attended Catholic School through eighth grade. For high school, she attended and graduated from Orangeburg Wilkinson High School. While in high school, Anjelica was a Cheerleader, which was a decision based on her desire to be a part of something. She later earned her Bachelor's Degree in Special Education from South Carolina State University. She began working at a few schools in South Carolina. She later returned to the Bronx to take care of my maternal grandmother until her passing. During that time, she completed her Master's Degree in School Administration from Mercy College. Anjelica also met her husband Joel, who is both Dominican and Panamanian. From their union, they have two beautiful daughters, Amaris and Arielle. They currently still live in the Bronx.

Janese, the second eldest sibling and middle child, also attended Holy Trinity Catholic School until middle school. There was an accident that occurred, in which my mother was not notified. This resulted in the transition into public school as, frankly, it doesn't look good to show out in front of the church's people. Janese attended Brookdale Middle School and Orangeburg Wilkinson

High School. While in high school, she was a member of the Volleyball Team and the well-respected Bruinette Basketball Team. Upon graduating high school, she attended the University of North Carolina at Charlotte, majoring in Nutrition. She attended until the second semester of her sophomore year, when she went to raise her first child, Imani, with her high school sweetheart. After returning to Orangeburg, Janese started her career and soon moved into the management ranks. She married her high school sweetheart and later gave birth to her second-born, Jamari. To seek life again outside of Orangeburg, the family moved to Franklin, Virginia, in a plan that would bring all the siblings together. She continued to build upon her management experience while in Virginia and expanded her family by giving birth to her youngest son, Javon. After a couple of years in Virginia, Janese and her family moved back to Orangeburg, where she became a single mother. Nothing short of what she had already done, she continued to provide for her family and rise to an Area Manager in her display of perseverance and diligence.

A minority family in both New York and Orangeburg has a significant meaning. My father grew up in Orangeburg around the Civil Rights Movement. He had recalled times when they had to pick cotton but would often cheat the system by putting rocks in the bucket's bottom to get the weight up. Another time I've heard he and my uncles describe it as the Orangeburg Massacre. On February 8, 1968, there was a massacre on the campus of South Carolina State. The collegiate students, and those in the local community, including my father and uncles, sought to desegregate All-Star Bowling, where the owner felt inclined to not comply with the Civil Rights Act of 1964. The tensions of that night mounted over three days when the South Carolina Highway Patrolmen fired upon the crowd, killing three students and wounding countless others.

The deceased's names were Samuel Hammond Jr., Delano Middleton, and Henry Smith, whereas Middleton was still in high school. The current gym on the campus is named after these young men in memory of the sacrifices from that night. While my family went home for curfew before the events unfolded, they still can recount the movement in their hometown.

New York could be considered a place where people went to come up with a hustle and make money. It's referenced as the city that never sleeps for a reason. While many rush to the city for financial gain, others move South to raise their families. My parents were working in Manhattan but eventually had to commute to Long Island, as the office had moved locations. Furthermore, an increase in crime and the emergence of the 'Crack Era' in the early 80s affected the city. With three kids, the decision was made to move to the South as others had done. While they had no jobs, the security of being able to move into one of the family homes helped. My uncle and aunt had lived there previously, so the timing worked out. The leftovers from the cafeteria on campus provided us with some meals. My parents made it work with family support and could get jobs. My father worked as an insurance agent at Liberty Life, while my mother found a job at C&S Bank next door.

I previously noted that background aids in my world's perceptions. Still, my experiences also play a significant role in my path. These experiences are deeply rooted in the notion of family. As mentioned, my father's side of the family is large. Most of my holidays and family events were spent at my grandmother's house on Sunnyside. We grew up in what is noted as 'The Reservations' in Orangeburg; we had to be creative in many things we did. It wasn't the best neighborhood, but it was home. We had extended family that lived one house down from us, and we were the crew growing up. When we were young, aside from riding bikes and playing games, we would play and tell jokes to one another. An example of these jokes would be, "your momma has one leg longer than the other and they call her I-Lean (Aileen)." Cruel and corny at the same time, I know. Some of our pranks were set out to give what was once referenced as the dumb face. We would do things such as tie another person's shoes together, so if they would try to walk, they would fall. While this would make the person mad, we knew revenge would be due. I was the recipient of most of the pranks since I was the youngest, slowest, and least experienced at the tricks and games. It made me think ahead and be ready for what was to come.

We also played kickball–one of America's favorite childhood games growing up. During the monotonous days of summer, rain or shine, our young, creative minds allowed us to play. Most times, we played outside, or if it were raining outside, we would play at our house or one house down with the crew. I'm sure there is curiosity as to how. We did not have vast houses and often pondered this same question as adults. Our houses were similar in design, and the top of the hallway would always be home; the bathroom was first base, the closet door in the hallway was second base, and the first bedroom on the left was third base. The score was always close, since the halls were too small. We would attempt to score by making the ball bounce off the walls while it bought time for someone to reach the base. The bushes and trees were used as bases if we could play outside, and the driveway was home. Since I was the youngest and not the fastest, I was usually the one to get out. With this game, we created rules as we went along. One of those rules was 'Ghost Man' where the person who was about to kick could call Ghost Man and be allowed to go to first base without being hit by the ball or counted out. This may sound crazy, but we made it work. We also played Hide and Go Seek and Freeze Tag, alongside Uno, I Declare War, and hand games. Basketball was also a favorite for some of us. The games taught us how to be victorious and live through defeat.

My sister Janese played a part in most of my most memorable punishments, while they were not all solely earned but shared with her. One instance is when she dared me to call 911 as we waited for my grandmother's flight to arrive from New York. This was the era of payphones, so my father had to call my aunt in New York to ensure my grandmother made her flight. My sister and I played on the payphones and inserted the dare as he was doing this. After dialing the first two digits, I looked over to her before hitting the last, where she smiled and cheered me on to do it. The phone quickly rang, and I heard the operator stating, "911. What's your emergency?" I immediately hung up the phone and celebrated my victory in the challenge. To my ignorance, they sent a police officer to the area where he questioned my father. With us being the only ones around, it was easy to conclude it was either my sister or me. Janese was all too helpful in helping him figure out the mystery. I took the verbal thrashing at the time since the officer's presence limited how much discipline could be given. As not already embarrassing enough, Janese felt compelled to tell my grandmother the whole story.

Another instance with my partner in crime came not far from home. My partner in crime gave me my most underserved punishment yet. One night, we waited outside in the car of our family's house. We spent just as much time at as our own. My mother went inside to get Anjelica, leaving Janese and me in the car. While waiting, Janese seemingly acquired knowledge of operating a vehicle and said, "Mommy has the car in the wrong gear." I know, yikes! After saying that, she reached from the backseat toward the steering wheel and pulled the gear down. The car rolled backward until we hit some trees in the woods across the street. We were both crying inside the car as other cars passed. They drove slowly, wondering if they should help, but we just waved them on to keep moving. Soon, the adults realized what had happened, and we were retrieved from the woods. My mother asked how it happened. As I was trying to explain that Janese had moved the car, Janese interrupted and blamed me. I was in complete and utter shock, as this was one time I had no part of what was done out of line. Unable to take sides and decipher who was responsible, my mother told us to wash and get in bed. I had done some naughty things in the past, and it was not beneath me, but this was not hard for me to deny involvement.

Crying uncontrollably, I asked my sister why she didn't tell the truth, and she said nothing in response. Unbeknownst to us, this was not the end of the issue. Janese and I got a spanking that night, and that is using the word nicely. The only benefit was that my mother didn't tell my father, as we were in his much-loved blue Oldsmobile Cutlass Supreme. It wasn't until we were older that Janese revealed her part, but it's like pulling teeth to get her to come clean again. Life is filled with memorable times and those we choose to forget from punishments, but this is the reality of the consequences of our choices.

All my upbringing was also not doom and gloom as we were exposed to living outside of Orangeburg and New York. We often traveled to vacation in Georgia, where Six Flags was a favorite, and Florida, where Wet' N Wild tops my list. Disney World was also on the list, but I am not a fan favorite. We also took day trips to Carowinds in North Carolina. We took several trips to Charleston, South Carolina, to Frankie's Fun Park while visiting family. While these were all fun endeavors, we saw the beauty of visiting Tennessee and seeing the mountains and Canada while attending a family reunion in Detroit. From a cultural experience, we visited the Dr. Martin Luther King, Jr. National Historical Park and King Center in Atlanta, Georgia, and the Biltmore Estate in Buncombe County, North Carolina. My parents tried to ensure we got to experience life outside of Orangeburg to broaden our outlook.

So, after giving the background of my immediate family and experiences, we are a diverse group. Born to a Catholic raised New York-born and bred mother and an African Methodist Episcopal (AME) raised South Carolinian father. This melting pot of ethnicities and experiences helps to form my foundation and beliefs of showing love to everyone regardless of affiliation, being competitive, and setting my sights high. My parents later went back to college. My father earned his Bachelor's Degree in Humanities, mainly focused on Divinity, from Allen University. My mother earned her Bachelor's and Master's Degrees in Criminal Justice from Claflin University and Troy University, respectively. My mother has evolved professionally and personally from working in banks and supervisory roles to now being in the field where she pursued her education. My father is a preacher who is quick to remind people he hasn't always been one. This is unapologetically me.

Chapter 2
Educational Start

My early school days began at Holy Trinity Catholic School in Orangeburg, South Carolina. The thought of just walking through the doors of a new environment sent my heart straight to my stomach as I approached the school's doors. The appearance of fresh faces and the unique experience of being away from my nursery left me speechless, which was almost impossible since I have always been a talker.

As I walked through the doors, I squeezed my mother's hand tighter. The transition from a nursery school to an actual school with multiple grade levels left me extremely nervous. Since most of the kids there were in preschool together, it was a comfortable change for them. As for me, I had to meet new people. My previous exposure at the daycare was to kids who looked like me and had similar interests; however, my new school had various kids with differing ethnicities. It wasn't wholly unfamiliar as my time in New York and the Catholic Church demonstrated an array of ethnic backgrounds.

Nevertheless, I watched other kids talk and laugh with each other after orientation was over. My mother encouraged me to speak with the other kids, but that was not a step I was prepared to take at that moment. Eventually, a girl walked over to me and introduced herself. I reluctantly spoke back in a shy manner, and soon enough, we were laughing and playing. I had so much fun that I didn't realize my mother had left. When it was time for all students to report to class, I relaxed and was ready to learn. As I walked into the classroom, I was greeted by my new teacher and could sit by my new friend the entire day. My first day didn't turn out to be so bad after all. I was so excited that as soon as I got in the car to go home, I couldn't stop telling my mother about my day. I realized it is normal to be afraid in a new place, but being open is even scarier. It is then that someone could end up missing out on a lot.

When I transitioned into a public school in the second grade, I started at Whittaker Elementary. There was a similar foundation regarding learning, but the students once again mostly resembled me. Whittaker was one of the better elementary schools relatively close to where I grew up. I met one of my lifelong best friends during this time and experienced my first fight. It was with a boy and came because of a disagreement I was having with my best friend. The guy had nothing to do with it, but felt compelled to be a part of it. I had dropped my keys, which went to nothing, by the way, and when I reached for them, I was met with a sneak punch in the nose. I don't know if you would even call it a fight since it was one-sided, and I didn't realize we were going there.

Nonetheless, it was enough to break my nose and send me to the emergency room. The rumors associated with what people perceived to have happened were entertaining and full of imagination, mostly from people who weren't even in the room. I returned to school the next day and resolved any issues with my best friend. That experience taught me that people are willing to fight against you regardless of their direct involvement with you. Also, people will develop their own narratives. Still, it is essential to stay the course and continue with your own story.

My middle school years included time at Brookdale Middle School primarily, but allowed me to spend one year at Howard Middle School because of admittance into the Gifted and Talented Program. It was fantastic to have friends at both schools and even more enjoyable during the rival athletic events. As I entered my fifth-grade year, my sister Janese was in the eighth grade. At that moment, I was Janese's little sister and had seemingly lost any name recognition. This is the casualty of being at the same school as an older sibling. It could've been worst, but she looked out for me during this time and allowed me to sometimes hang with her and her friends. She probably had little choice, but I felt like she was willing if I didn't embarrass her. I injured my knee during the school year and had to wear a straight-leg knee brace. One of my classmates picked on me as I received an award during our Honors and Awards Program. It bothered me to the point it bothered Janese. She tried to track this guy down in the cafeteria from multiple entrances, only to finally be stopped by an administrator. This was a perk of one of my big sister being at the same school as me, from a somewhat rival to a sure partner in crime.

I understood the true meaning of being a student-athlete in middle school. We could not do any extracurricular activities if our grades were not in order. I graduated middle school with the third-highest grade point average in the class and the highest average in my Algebra I class. I was taking high school courses in eighth grade to obtain high school credits earlier. Once I entered high school at Orangeburg Wilkinson, the familiar pattern of losing my name took place again. I was now Janese's little once again. However, I came into my own, but I am not sure if you ever lose the identity of your siblings.

While in high school, I got my first job working at the local Piggly Wiggly, making a whopping $5.15. Yes, you read that correctly, and I was super proud of that and felt some sense of independence. I started working at fifteen and honestly have done nothing but in some capacity since. I felt more of a sense of responsibility and learned some aspects of professionalism. Also, I had to maintain a schedule and budget my checks. Later, I worked at Winn-Dixie and followed in the shoes of my older sister, Anjelica.

While working, I also maintained my status as a student-athlete. I became a member of Who's Who Among American High School Students, the National Honor Society, Key Club, Section Leader for the Percussion Section in the Orangeburg Wilkinson High School' Orange Pride' Band, and Orangeburg Wilkinson High School Girls Basketball Team known as the 'Bruinettes'. During this time, the band had been ranked number four in the state, and the Brunettes were the 2000 Region Three, Class 4A State Basketball Champions. I grew up watching Bruinette Basketball, and that blood ran through my veins. I saw several young ladies play with confidence and authority, which fed my competitive spirit. The motto of our beloved coach was, "Where winning is not a habit—it's a tradition." It was here that I hungered to win, not just in sports but in life. I graduated number 13 out of 266 in my class. I received an academic scholarship to North Carolina A&T State University in Greensboro, North Carolina.

Graduation placed upon me an onus of being a young adult, the reflection of friendships made and lost, experiences with valuable lessons, and goals that I accomplished. Each graduation introduced new chapters in my life.

I decided on attending North Carolina A&T for several reasons, with the first being the top producer of black engineers in the country. I had acquired an interest in computers and electronics because of the influence of my grandfather. What better place to cultivate my path? Also, my family was avid South Carolina State supporters, and it allowed me to see many HBCUs (Historically Black Colleges and Universities). That placed Florida A&M in the running, but I was sold on the engineering part. It also helped that another one of my best friends had attended the year prior.

I ran to Greensboro from Orangeburg, not knowing what was ahead. Heck, I didn't even know how to properly shop as a college student, but I was grateful to have my best friend and her parents assist me in making value price comparisons. I was admitted into the Computer Science program but soon learned after my first year that I did not have a strong interest in looking for missing semicolons in programming logic. My view has always been to walk my path, but hindsight, alongside my best friend's voice resonating, told me I should have majored in Electrical Engineering that would've been more in the realms of what I was seeking as a career path. Furthermore, I attempted to keep challenging myself and walked onto the basketball team. That was the fastest reminder of "you're doing too much" that I have ever received. I quickly learned it required a different rigor than I was willing to give at the time. My father told me he wasn't telling me what to do, but to remember who was paying for me to be there. This was a big step in maintaining responsibility as I left the game of basketball, which I loved, to focus on my studies.

The challenges of higher education varied from back home, as I felt like some of the other students must have had a head start over me. One day, I even walked in the rain, thinking I would lose my scholarship and be sent home. My best friend offered me a ride, but I refused. I felt only worthy to walk in the rain. I was met with the constant challenges of limited text messages and minutes, with free calls only after 9 pm, which eventually moved to 7 pm. I was under my mother's phone plan and felt I was grown by this time. I did not want to hear the constant lecture about the phone bill, so I cut off my phone and relied only on the phone in my room until I could afford a cellular phone. In my push to have the responsibility, I transferred my job at Winn Dixie in Orangeburg to the one in Greensboro. It wasn't in the best area, and I wasn't sure how I was getting to and from work, but I made it work. It also helped to have the friends from Orangeburg either attending the same school or close by and a family we adopted while we were there. This at least helped me to go home if I wanted and chip in on the gas and driving responsibility.

I returned home the summer of my freshman year and worked at Winn Dixie in the mornings, took a class at South Carolina State, and worked at Video Warehouse under the management of Janese in the afternoons and nights. One would think working for your sister would provide some benefit, but she worked me! Of course, she left all the menial tasks to me but would beg to differ when I bring this up. I worked that summer to prepare for a car but realized I had no credit. I tried to not fall for the pitfalls my sisters told me about with applying for credit cards to get a t-shirt or meal, but it left me with few options for credit. My grandmother went out on a limb for me and co-signed on a car. I'm not sure why, as I still had not secured a job in Greensboro for the upcoming year, but she clearly had more faith in me than I did. I got a job tutoring other students when I went back…thank you, God! This allowed me to cover my car note and insurance and use my refund from housing to secure an off-campus apartment with my best friend. God made a way and gave me the support of my sisters when I didn't have it. Anjelica would send me money here and there, and Janese met me with the money to join Delta Sigma Theta Sorority, Incorporated. I had to choose between my responsibilities and paying my initiation fees. She made it where I didn't have to decide because she knew how much I wanted to be a part of such an illustrious organization. We still joke about her being honorary because of coming through for me. My parents were not wealthy, but we had what we needed growing up. I tried not to ask them for much, but my sisters clearly had a sixth sense of when I needed help.

While working in the Engineering Department, I continued to maintain my studies. I learned so much from this role as I could through interacting with professionals at corporations on behalf of my supervisor. He challenged me to grow in the aspects of business, as well as allowed me to work outside of that position to earn extra money. This was helpful, as I stayed in Greensboro that summer, received a scholarship and laptop, and attended classes during the summer. This allowed me to be poised as I entered my junior year and continued tutoring and working in the Engineering Department.

In the summer of my junior year, I was awarded an internship for a reputable computer company in DuPont, Washington. I knew nothing about the state of Washington, nor knew of anyone living there. The only person remotely close to that side of the country was my mother's sister. My paternal grandmother was not thrilled about the opportunity. She felt I had no business going that far away from home alone. Yet, the desire to take risks and accept challenges had not left my spirit; therefore, off to Washington, I went. After traveling from my first plane ride, I took a cab to where I had found housing. Housing suggestions were provided by the company where employees listed their space. It was nothing like I had imagined, and I was unsure of the living conditions upon seeing my home for the summer. For the summer, my landlord and roommate stated he would not be there when I arrived, but there was another male roommate unbeknownst to me. I went to take a shower and was displeased by the bathroom and hair everywhere. I then went to what was my room and went to lock the door, only to realize the lock did not work. Also, the house was freezing! What the hell had I gotten myself into? I slept horribly, as I still needed all my senses to be in tack. The following day, I hurried to see what was in the surrounding area since I had left my car at home on the East Coast. I found a popular sandwich shop that would be my place to dine, due to limited transportation options. My job would be a little less than a mile away, which was reasonable. Although my landlord worked at the company, I had yet to meet him or the other person in the house.

The following morning, I was off to work as it drizzled. During this walk, I thought I would just return home and work at the video store again if needed. I met my manager and those in the department, but noticed no one looked like me. Not another African American or female, aside from the Administrative Assistants. It seemed like the work would be interesting. However, I still felt doubtful about my ability to endure the living conditions. I had discussed this with my family and was prepared to look for a ticket and head home. The next day, I went to work but still had not met the people I was living with and could not address the lock on the door.

At lunch, I sat in the cafeteria, thinking I would finish the week out and inform them I would no longer finish my internship when an African American man approached me. He said, "You must be Janelle." Since I don't hide my facial expressions very well, he already sensed my thought about who you are and how you know who I am. He told me his name and said he knew who I was because they announced I was coming and there weren't many 'sistas' around. I felt some relief and was introduced to people who looked like me that afternoon. That afternoon, I learned what an affinity group was and understood the need. This kind man then extended an offer to show me around and eat dinner with him and his wife. I should've been skeptical, but felt relief based on what I had endured in feeling lonely for the past couple of days. Dinner with them was outstanding, and I expressed to them my initial taste of Washington. As he took me back to my living quarters, we stopped by their house, and he gave me a comforter to take with me so I wouldn't be cold. I didn't hesitate as I was sleeping fully clothed with a hoodie pulled over my head and no store in walking distance. He also mentioned asking his wife about me renting a room from them. The next day, he found me and told me she agreed. This was also the first day my landlord was at work. I met him to tell him I would not be staying there and to pay him for the week. He seemed confused but understood after I explained the circumstances.

My newfound Washington family was what I needed to endure during the summer. From a professional aspect, I met a couple of other people and learned the phases of corporate organizations from my new family, helping me to acclimate to the environment; likewise, his wife showed me facets of being a businesswoman. I was fortunate enough to meet both families and indulged in several family meals. There were some Southern ties within the family, so the meals were more than fitting for my appetite. I also learned to water tube that summer and spent some time with them on the boat. There were countless times I ended up falling off and into the water while even ripping some shorts on one go. It wasn't until I was about to leave that he told me the secret to staying on the tube.

Furthermore, I visited and captured images of Mount Rainier alongside my best friend, who visited. One photo I took was even published in a book. This was another cultural awakening as I toured Seattle and the infamous Pike Place Market and even went to Canada with my new family.

Being on the West Coast, I got to go to Vegas for my sorority's, Delta Sigma Theta, national convention. Vegas heat is like no other and not even comparable to South Carolina's. It was a dry heat, and I felt it on my skin immediately after getting off the plane. It was exciting as I could see some familiar faces and meet up with my line sisters and some of our big sisters from the chapter. This sense of family was what I needed to get through the summer, but the ultimate fulfillment came on my 21st birthday. I had planned to go visit my aunt in California since she was the closest relative to me on the West Coast, and this would give me a chance to take a trip since I had never been. My older sister, Anjelica, would meet me there to help me celebrate, as I think she knew how much I had missed them.

Janese wouldn't be able to make the trip due to work and taking care of her young daughter. As I eagerly got off the plane in California, I sought my aunt and Anjelica as they were picking me up. Once I saw them, we hugged ridiculously and were full of excitement and relief. I then looked over and saw another familiar face. It was Janese! We're not the crying type, but the moment brought on tears and joy. I have a special bond with my sisters, so the moment was immense. The tone alone of my conversations over the phone must have let them know just how much I missed them. I had met a new family that had taken me in as their own, but the ability to see those that knew me best meant the world to me. Janese said it was hard not to say anything to us since we spoke frequently. She had arrived first earlier that morning and surprised Anjelica as well. My aunt was the only one that knew she was coming. We spent the weekend together, taking in California, Universal Studios, and dinner with some of my aunt's friends. This allowed some ease into the rest of my days in Washington.

The experience continued to pour into me and my viewpoint on life. My Washington family provided me with the comfort I felt while growing up by inviting me into their realm and broadened me as I continued to evolve as a woman. It was hard when it was time for me to leave because of the rapport built with them. They even knew all about my family back home and even met my father when they visited Georgia. It was funny because she would call me Ga-nelle, which my niece Imani would call me as she struggled to say my name correctly when she was younger. He understood my love for sports as we played basketball during lunch at work and rushed to catch the NBA playoffs after work. I didn't realize there was a basketball court there and didn't prepare; thus, I played in my Chuck Taylors. These are not the same shoes they played basketball in during their early years. As a result, I busted through their side while playing one day and had to improvise from there.

We went to dinner my last night at the same place they took me to my first night. When I headed to the airport, I found out my flight had been canceled. This gave me another night to spend with them and made me anxious to reunite with my family. I even requested to be picked up in my car, 'The Pro Pro', which I had worked for and not driven since I left. My time over the summer was something I did not take for granted, and I still maintained contact with my Washington family.

When I returned for my senior year, I saw the light at the end of the tunnel. All of what I had worked to achieve was coming to fruition. I was then left with the decision to go to graduate school or enter the workforce. During my journey of trying to figure it out, I took action to set myself up for both. It was always crucial for me to have a contingency plan. I applied for the GEM Fellowship that my best friend had received the year earlier. This would allow me to work on my Master's in Engineering on a full academic scholarship, but I also applied for several jobs. The fellowship was awarded to me as well as being offered a job. I wasn't sure I wanted to continue down the engineering path. Still, I knew I wanted to further my education based on the continued advice of my grandparents. It was fortunate that the company I was seeking employment with offered tuition reimbursement. As a result, I went to work and would seek a graduate degree after getting practical experience. I graduated from North Carolina A&T with Magna Cum Laude honors and began my career. The experience afforded by attending such a prestigious HBCU can never be replaced and embodies a sense of pride, Aggie Pride, if I say so myself!

Chapter 3
Entering Corporate America

When I began my role in Corporate America, I wasn't sure what to expect. I knew what I had learned during my internship, reviewed some professional development items from Career Services, and even reflected on the professionals I knew around me and how they presented themselves. I wasn't sure what I was supposed to be doing or how I would contribute. Nonetheless, I wanted to start my professional journey the way I had done throughout life. I brought an open mind and undying willingness to learn, alongside competitiveness, authenticity, and transparency. There were some aspects of professional appearance I was suggested to follow, such as removing the piercings at the top of my ears. Still, the company was getting authentically the person I presented in the interview.

As with any company, you have introductory training to acclimate you to your new organization. Some of these were not surprising, but there were a couple that I was unsure about; however, they have proved to be more valuable than I realized then. One piece of training was an etiquette course while eating. I thought it was unnecessary and strange, but it was something I had not been privy to experiencing. The instructor coached us on certain foods that should be avoided at a business dinner, alongside which silverware to use and when. It even went down to how to cut your food should cutting be required. This was good information, and we even put it to practice over lunch. The only bad thing I could recall was it was over lunch, and I was starving! I was told to hold off and slow down when all I wanted was to devour my food. In my mind, I would practice slowing down when I truly needed to do so. This training stuck with me.

Another training I was exposed to was presentation skills. Of course, I had given presentations in school, particularly for my Senior Design course; yet this was different, as the content wasn't as important as the body language conveyed. We covered the usual training, encompassing doing presentations and presenting using PowerPoint. We were then challenged to deliver a presentation using a piece of paper from a flip chart. The presentation was based on a random object we were given, where my object was Play-Doh. How could I talk for an allotted timeframe about Play-Doh? This sparked some creativity alongside being mindful of my voice, pace, and hand motions. While seemingly an irrelevant exercise, I prepared myself for what the future held full of audiences who would be interested in what I had to say. This would have to be done by keeping their attention and not allowing distractions because of unnecessary movements.

These were trainings I didn't expect or knew I needed. I was also given a female mentor and was given traveling tips and guidance on being in the plant alongside the other female engineers. This was another exposure to diversity that I didn't quite catch. While the organization was working on diversifying, I didn't realize there were still pitfalls that were important to understand being a female functioning in a male-dominated industry. There was information on selecting indoor access hotels instead of outdoor access hotels because of safety concerns.

We were informed of appropriate workplace behavior and what was tolerable and terminable behavior. Hence, although being female, catcalling from our male peers is not permitted. I thought these were obvious but still crucial for the company to emphasize as changes in the workforce continued to evolve, particularly with the number of females increasing. I traveled for the first year to different sites doing projects. This information was helpful without me recognizing the need to state what should be obvious.

After traveling for shy of a year, I was placed at a mutually aligned location with myself and the site. In my new role, I was a sponge. I wanted to absorb everything available to learn about the process, but focused on working with people. I built a rapport with people throughout the plant as I evolved in my career. My projects allowed me to use some creativity to find solutions and contribute to the long-term path for the reliability of operations. While I had momentum and enthusiasm behind me, I didn't want to lose sight of furthering my educational endeavors. I began working on my Master of Business Administration (MBA) while I worked. The practical experiences gave me significant content for the assignments and papers I had to write. During this time, I was also promoted to my first supervisory role. The makeup of the team was much like that of the site. There was a generational mix, but gender lacked diversity, and there was only one minority that reported to me. This was the challenge of a young black female leading a predominantly white male team.

With my new team, I brought my tools previously mentioned of a willingness to learn, competitiveness, authenticity, and transparency. Teamwork would be equally important, and I wanted them to see me as a part of the team. In doing so, it was imperative to not compromise who I was and establish boundaries. With any team, statistics for efficiency were vital. We evaluated how successful we were at completing tasks. I even came up with an award for the most efficient group within the team. I also listened to them but made sure it made sense and wasn't meant to get over on me. I was always taught to validate and not merely to go off the strength of what is being said. We didn't always agree, but showed up to perform when needed. It was also a part of my upbringing that one person's role is no more significant than the next. One example is when we had a product freeze on the lines. It was cold that night trying to get the line to thaw, but I felt obliged to stay with my team. I even joined in with the attempts to soften the line, which I was not supposed to do, but they allowed. It was probably because it was freezing, and I was another set of hands to keep the efforts going. This wasn't done for recognition but contributed to my innate drive to exude teamwork. One of my guys told me I had 'testicular fortitude' based on my leadership approach. While this could have been one boundary, I'm not that sensitive and knew his intent. I had grown up playing basketball with boys in my neighborhood in my early years and was familiar with such verbiage.

As I continued to thrive in my role, the Plant Manager took notice and the Maintenance Manager. I was asked to go recruiting back at North Carolina A&T to recruit others like me. When I first heard this, I was taken aback and initially thought this would make me a token. However, my wise best friend presented an alternative viewpoint of not being a token but bringing those along that might have otherwise been overlooked. I was the example of what could be for those who looked like me to help diversify the company's efforts. You should have friends who don't just go along with what you think, which helps create a good balance for yourself. As a result, I began my stint in recruiting.

Things were going well, and I had completed school. My Plant Manager continued to take note and exposed me to the world of golf. I had no interest in golf, and though it was not an exciting sport. My dad informed me that significant discussions and deals happen on the golf course. I bought my first set of clubs and prepared to participate. This should be doable because I was an athlete and am still active. I played on the team with the Plant Manager, a female, and I sucked! This was an opportunity for me to learn again and understand the Plant Manager and her path. It also helped that we had some refreshments available as we played.

This networking opportunity went well, and I received a company award. I started mentoring relationships with her and a couple of other managers in the plant. I was moving into another supervisory role in a new area. However, this had culminated with the decision to close the site. It was heartbreaking as the news passed throughout the plant and to see the impact of those whose lives and families were embedded there and in the community over several years. I was, fortunately, able to move to another site within the company. However, I still felt attached to the place where it all started for me professionally. Not to mention another family I had become acquainted with and became family away from my own. I could move back closer to home. If another facility closed, I figured I could always stay with my mother or father.

Chapter 4
You Need More Development

When I arrived at my new site, I had taken a reduced role and became an individual contributor. This assured me I would at least be close to home and my family should something occur, such as another closure. There was more diversity among females and managers at this location, and there was still a sense that the group of minorities ensured there was a supportive environment for one another. I developed a friendship with two females, who were young and black as well. These were confident and ambitious women who displayed alpha female traits like me. We discussed our ambitions, challenges, and got to know each other's families. This was the most welcoming aspect of being there, but their battles resembled my own. One was a member of Generation X, while the other was a Millennial; still, we differed only by age as our experiences in having to do and be more were the same.

Like other professional experiences, there was traction in forming affinity groups. There was one that targeted not only African Americans but also women. There was an identification of the need for minorities overall to have a voice in a formalized manner. These representations would be key in providing an avenue for other minorities and seeking to form some sort of alliance in giving a voice. This location was known for typically building from within, so this would be a challenge to fully implement the change these groups sought.

In my new location, I didn't quite feel at home as in my previous location. I took on the assignments that were given to me, but I still aspired to get back into the managerial ranks. I attempted to do so by applying for a position in the technical realm. However, I was not awarded the position. Although I had some competencies listed in the posting and could build effective teams, I lacked ten years of experience. Within the ten years of experience, the posting manager was looking for a proven track record of building effective teams and the experiences that came along with the successes and the failures of doing so.

Seemingly, nothing I had done at my previous location was relevant, and I was starting from the beginning of my career again. While it was mentioned I demonstrated signs of management talent, there could potentially be an opportunity later in a supervisory role, but not for the role to which I had applied. A good leader was needed to manage a program as opposed to people. While this was what I was currently doing, it wasn't fulfilling. Not to mention, the person who received the position I had applied for had an Associate's Degree in the Arts, and no technical background. Unfortunately, this was the first conversation in the eight months of my being there regarding my aspirations. This was a huge wake-up for me to take control of my career. My manager didn't realize I wasn't locked into one career path, nor my desire to be in the thick of things making it happen. It wasn't until then; I noticed getting my MBA in General Management didn't resonate loud enough I was open to professional growth. Not to mention, I continued my recruiting activities on behalf of the company.

I wanted to ensure I was versatile in my career and gained experiences outside of my current career path. If the plant closure taught me anything, it was not to have all your eggs in one basket. I refused to stop there and sought more feedback from management. I soon entered a production management role focused on processes. This differed from my technical experience and provided me with an opportunity to manage a team where I had no people directly reporting to me. This was different, and I accepted the challenge. However, after a year, it still didn't feel right. I communicated to the person who hired me I didn't think this was a fit. I also spoke to my direct manager, the HR Manager, and the Plant Manager about my concerns. These three individuals were all white males, belonging to Generation X, who could not understand what I was looking for, nor me. I got the impression I just should have appreciated what was being offered to me.

The initial meeting was between my manager and the HR Manager to discuss career planning. This was premised on feedback from a one-on-one meeting with my manager where I got feedback. I sought clarification to some of the information provided, as I wanted to ensure I took heed to the feedback. The leadership gave me a "Meets Commitment" and stated I needed to learn more technical detail in certain areas of the plant. Based on my aspirations and current role, I posed the question regarding intricacy referring to the equipment and tried to understand the intent of the message provided by the leadership team. My manager could not answer the questions as he stated he did not attend the meeting, but the HR Manager had attended on his behalf. The HR Manager then noted it was so long ago, he could not remember where the comment came from and couldn't explain what was meant by the comment. In my head, I'm thinking…what??? Again, my facial expressions reveal my sentiments. The generic response I was provided after that was to take advantage of every learning opportunity while in my current role.

Because of this confusing and unresolved meeting, I pursued information on a career plan. Seemingly, there was a misunderstanding of my career aspirations amongst the leadership, with my desire to be fluid in career planning with being open to a manufacturing position, a support role, or a technical function. However, this was not a new discussion as it was previously held with my manager as he focused on my degrees in engineering and business. In being consistent with exposing myself to all opportunities, I indicated that my interest was not limited to one set path, and I wanted to keep my options open depending on the potential role. Not that I was willing to accept anything, but there needed to be mutual alignment where it would benefit me and the organization. I was very deliberate in ranking my preferences for opportunities as not to appear indecisive.

Companies in Corporate America are huge, and you don't know what you don't know. It was reiterated to me again during this meeting that no one knew what my interest and goals were, yet I referenced discussions I've had with those in varying tiers of leadership either through one-on-ones or through feedback provided after putting in for an open position. It was deemed, then, that what I had listed as prospective career options was adequate in my profile;

however, it was noted by the HR Manager stating opportunities are few and far in between as people would be promoted through the ranks and some development roles are slated for other managers. Translation...don't hold your breath!

The opportunities for me at the site seemed limited, but mainly because it was structured that way. My previous manager at my prior facility reached out to me regarding a management position at the facility where he had moved. This plant would be an hour and a half drive from where I lived, but I would make it work just to get my career back on track. It left me to pose two questions: 1) Was I releasable? 2) How am I qualified for a position at another plant, but not locally? This was met with more smoke and mirrors. It was mentioned the locations differ and I should be patient. Conversely, patience is not one of my stronger traits.

If I stayed the technical management route, I would have to wait on an opening through attrition; however, this path would be difficult as I was already told by the manager informally that I did not fit the criteria for the role there compared to what I had already done at my previous plant. After hearing this, the HR Manager finally stated it wouldn't be impossible, but would be competitive through the ranks.

This led to the realization I would need to transfer out to continue to progress in my career. Additionally, I let it be known that I did not feel there was an advocate representing my interest, nor did I feel a part of any discussion about progression and contingency planning. The HR manager mentioned he would discuss it with the Plant Manager as he might have confused some things. Nonetheless, I would need to wait and communicate any changes at the beginning of the year and was encouraged not to have too frequent meetings to get my interest conveyed. I wondered if it was too frequent, or they were uncomfortable with me being vocal about my interests and lack of support?

I sought additional assignments to aid in my development, both internally and externally. A suggestion posed by the HR Manager was I take leadership classes and other courses at a local technical college. Again, the gears in my head turned as I was confused about what I was to gain from the technical college that I had not in acquiring my MBA. No offense to technical schools, as they are essential for trades and competency development, but had these meetings been meaningless? Did they still not understand my background? Frustrating is a mild way to put this experience.

Up next were limitations in my pay level and their anticipation I wouldn't be in the role long enough to move up in the level structure. I was not only limited in roles but also financially constrained. This couldn't be real as the messages were mixed with being patient, with the insistence I wouldn't be in the role long enough.

Along the way, I found out the plant got credit for exporting talent. While I was not good enough for where I was currently, I could perform at other locations while my current location took credit for my development. There was an announcement of a promotion for one of my counterparts who was hired into the same program as I had been, but later. He was a white male with a similar background of an engineering degree and MBA in progress. Yet, the position he was awarded was never posted. I was told that it is up to the discretion of the Department Manager to post the job or not. Certainly, this was not an appropriate HR practice, but a means to deter me from applying. I thought about my exit strategy either with or without my current employer, as a sense of clarity was gained from these multiple meetings that seemed to want to keep me complacent and silenced.

I transferred to the other facility and was advocated for by a former peer and my previous manager. This new role enabled me to work with all facets of the plant and manage new engineers. It also allowed me to get additional training that was common in most industries, Greenbelt Training. Managing and mentoring younger engineers also allowed me to see where generational differences and upbringings varied from my own. There was no blanket to management, which I had already identified, but there was a true need for leadership as I further honed these skills.

While assuming this position, I was also an Assistant Coach for Varsity Girls' Basketball at my high school alma mater. This, too, allowed me to mentor young minds and examine the influence cultural upbringings have on people and their decisions. In both roles, I intended to challenge each person's mind to think beyond their world and immediate needs. I had no right or wrong answers, but wanted these individuals to evolve into being good humans.

The new opportunity allotted me support, development, and continued friendships. Yet, the commute, in conjunction with coaching and spending time with my paternal grandmother before her passing, caused quite a strain. I eventually left my employer for an opportunity with less of a commute. I appreciated all the experiences and growth to which I was exposed.

Chapter 5

Something "New"

As I left behind several years with my employer, I stepped out into a new opportunity. This was still in the realm of manufacturing, but different industry. I had taken a significant pay cut to be closer to home, but had the benefit of a shorter drive to visit my grandmother and help coach the team. This was the best decision, as nothing could replace the time I got to spend with my grandmother. When she was in her final moments, I made it there after receiving a phone call. Her ending was near. I sat beside her as she took her last breath. She was at peace and no longer in pain. This was something no amount of money could cover as I would not have made it there if I were still with my previous employer and left for an hour and a half drive.

This was a new opportunity ahead of me. The makeup of the other supervisors was mostly black persons belonging to Generation X, with management roles being held by white males and a few white females. I was put in training where I went through the entire process and did the work involved in the manufacturing method. It allowed me to meet different people in the departments and realized who was proficient in their jobs. Getting to know people was no longer a problem from my early years of school as I inherited the 'gift of gab' trait from my father's side of the family. We have never met a stranger and I probably could talk to a wall.

People there asked what I thought about the job up to that point, and what I was told regarding expectations. I told them the selling aspects of the job that got me there, as well as mentioned some overtime. The 'some overtime' comment was met with laughter as they stated they worked overtime all the time. I kept note, as this was not what was communicated. I continued my training, and in doing the actual work and talking to people, I grew a respect for those doing it daily. I had so many micro scratches from working on the line, I would be an OSHA recordable if they didn't get me into my job quickly.

As I learned the process, I learned my area and how we could be efficient. I took the processes currently in place and evaluated how to track job completion. This was prioritized based on due dates to the customer and the competencies of the technicians. Some technicians always wanted the complex jobs and demonstrated their ability to do so repeatedly, while some others had opportunities to improve. I sought opportunities to leverage the load and mix the skillsets of the team, where the most proficient people would work with some that required additional development. My approach was to balance the team appropriately, while I always strive to be fair to all and hold everyone accountable. This accountability is inclusive of me, and I wouldn't ask them to do anything I wouldn't do myself.

I grew confident in my role and increased consecutive months of on-time delivery with the team. My confidence in the role had grown to where I challenged those in meetings who sought to place blame on my team for any delays. The team took on challenges to make up the time for process delays, as well as went to help in other areas of the value stream so we could get work and adhere to deliver promise dates. We became so efficient that I worked to convince the leadership to get rid of the night shift in my department, as we would be even more productive on one shift. This would increase employee morale as those that were on nights were displeased with the schedule. With things going in the right direction, nothing could go wrong, right? Wrong! Interpersonal savvy, which I have also considered a strength of mine, would not be welcomed by all. A valuable lesson learned is not everyone will be comfortable with your confidence.

Things took a turn for the worst, possibly because I was working six to seven days a week sometimes. I had already taken a significant pay cut but didn't want to continue to diminish my value any further by working more. This took a toll on me and my job satisfaction. I lived approximately five minutes from my job but would show up at the very minute I had to be there, or somewhat later.

Things seemed to go well with the manager of the area, to which I did not directly report, but took a turn when I started pointing out delays from her team. This put a strain on my team and sometimes affects our ability to ship on time. During a one-on-one with my HR representative, I was asked how everything was going. I told her I wasn't sure this was the place for me and that I was breaking down. I disclosed issues with the manager, of which she seemed to be aware. Apparently, the two of them were friends, and she was already privy to some information the manager disclosed.

From now on, I communicated to the HR representative I would limit my discussions pertaining to work, as I felt there was a hidden agenda on behalf of the manager. Otherwise, this would adversely affect my job. Management also put additional resources in my area that weren't needed and only slowed the process because of their need for training. I was amid formally documenting our procedures but wasn't prepared to implement and streamline for effectiveness.

Because of my frustrations, I took the rest of the day to calm down and reflect. Later, I was to schedule a follow-up meeting with the HR representative to see how things were going. The meeting was to seek if there was anything to be done, which I conveyed there was not much that could be done. I had already taken a pay cut, so I wasn't motivated by money. However, I informed the HR representative that I felt the details of our conversation had been disclosed to the manager, as she seemed to be more persistent in targeting me. Naturally, she denied it and suggested I discuss the matter with my direct manager to aid in resolving it. In the interim, I sent my team leader to the production meetings to minimize my interactions with the manager with whom I was having problems.

At that point, I felt the issue would be handled by the managers and we would continue business as usual. Contrarily, a couple of weeks later, I met with my direct manager, who informed me a complaint had been formed in HR about my attitude and that I needed to adjust my behavior to preserve my career. This was a complete turn of events from what I was conveying to HR. My manager suggested I take on another position to get back some sort of work-life balance, while not having to worry about my situation with the other manager.

Of note, my manager at the time was a black female belonging to Generation X. Her manager was also a member of Generation X, but a white male. My manager was familiar with the struggles as a black female in the workforce, but had opted to take a different approach and not address things head-on. I reiterated some of the previous concerns detailed here and the concerns I was fighting to maintain my career. I informed her I would relay my decision to move to another role later. Later that evening, I incurred a medical issue where the doctor had taken me out of work for the following day. I took additional days as well to collect my thoughts on what was happening to me professionally.

I returned to work the following week and attempted to maintain a positive attitude, aside from being provoked by the manager upon my return. The next day, I had a meeting scheduled with the HR representative that afternoon, but it was moved up to that morning. When I arrived, the manager also showed up. I thought she had scheduled a meeting for the two of us to discuss our issues; however, the manager proceeded into the HR Manager's office with the Plant Manager.

We started our meeting in the room next door, but it was evident that she had been crying, as her eyes were puffy and red. She asked me how my relationship with the manager was going, and I informed her nothing had changed and that I only maintain contact with work-related issues. She also asked if I had considered taking another position, and I informed her I was not interested in doing so. I was not as engaged in this discussion and didn't expound upon my answers too much, as I had lost trust in any confidentiality within HR. I did, however, feel compelled to ask her what was wrong. She informed me she emailed something she shouldn't have sent, but she sent it out and there's nothing she can do. She told me there would be corrective actions and stated, "oh well." At that point, I realized the manager was being terminated next door to me, and I felt completely uncomfortable being up there based on our history.

After rationalizing and lining up the events that preceded the conversation about my attitude, I went to my manager the next day and stated that I felt as if I was being retaliated against by my comments made in HR. The confidentiality of that department had been compromised. I expressed my rationale for this thinking, which eventually led to the complaint being filed against me. My manager informed me HR initially wanted a meeting with full documentation to go into my file. She convinced them it was not required and that it would be handled. She didn't feel what was provided to HR would inhibit my career.

Later, I sent a letter to my manager requesting another HR representative for my team and myself. This was premised solely on recent concerns. Several weeks later, I was informed the HR Manager did not want to rotate my HR representative, as he planned to rotate them every year between groups to learn the business. However, I did not have to continue to meet on a one-on-one basis with my HR representative.

As time continued to pass, I had an employee who was terminated as he struck another employee back who hit him. I was told that the aggressor kept saying inappropriate things to my direct report and eventually pushed him. From this, a fight ensued. It was mentioned in statements. The other employee had a crazy look in his eyes and even attempted to hit others in the group with a drill as they were attempting to separate the two. I presented this information to the HR Manager and HR representative while informing them this was not to get my employee's termination rescinded but to understand the policy as I understood he was defending himself.

While discussing, I made a statement that I couldn't say that I wouldn't hit someone back if they maliciously hit me. They stated I should not as it would result in my job, but the HR representative did state that a similar comment was made by another manager. This led to further discussion and the need to have a Supervisor and

All-Employee meeting to discuss the policy and the consequences of violating the policy. They thanked me for my feedback and the conversation ended.

Later that evening, I called my manager to inform her that my doctor wanted me to adjust my working environment and remain off the production floor. I was informed there were concerns brought to her attention by HR. The HR representative was concerned with my comments made earlier that I would hypothetically hit someone back if I was involved in an altercation. As a result, she needed to discuss it with me. I questioned what was documented when the other manager made a similar statement, and how can I be documented for something supposititious that did not take place? I reminded my manager of our similar conversation earlier in the day where those things were stated. I added further that I didn't feel like I can succeed as I am being targeted for everything. I consulted other members of management about my concerns and issues. This resulted in them following up with the Plant Manager, who assured me not to worry as he was aware of the situation and had my back.

Other instances of chaos in an unhealthy environment continued in the upcoming months. There was a safety concern regarding job tasks in one of my areas of the assembly process. During the discussion, the Safety Manager stated she was unaware the associates were performing tasks in an unsafe manner. However, one of my direct reports stated he was told to "be careful" and "be safe" on a couple of occasions while performing the task. The method of this task was in place well before my tenure.

As frustration set in, the Safety Manager raised her voice and speak in a demeaning manner. She made a statement, "It's better than y'all crawling around the gear like a bunch of monkeys." For reference, the Safety Manager was a white female and either at the cusp of Generation X or Baby Boomer. The team members she was talking to were black males on the brink of being Millennials and Generation X. My associates then became disengaged, and one even pulled me to the side saying, "If she says that monkey shit again, I'm going to go off." She eventually told me she would not talk to me anymore because I was not in support of her suggestions.

At that moment, I did not touch on the insensitive verbiage used. The suggestions proposed also presented significant safety risks. To bring attention to the statement made and attempt to prevent a larger HR issue in the future, I informed my managers of the matter. They appeared to be disinterested in the comment made about the monkeys and questioned whether it should even be addressed. I suggested one of them proceed with a discussion as the Safety Manager may be unaware of how her comments could be interpreted and could cause future issues. To my knowledge, they did not follow up on the matter. I later informed another manager of the comments and was asked about my accounts of what happened, besides witnesses to the event. The Safety Manager came to me later and apologized for her actions and attempted to understand what the concerns were, which I educated her.

Weeks later, I returned from vacation to follow up with my manager regarding events occurring while I was out. There was corrective action that needed to be given to one of my direct reports while I was out. Prior to me taking a vacation, it was agreed upon to go forward with what was documented. The corrective action was not delivered as planned, as the associate had called out of work, which resulted in an additional corrective action for attendance. I was informed that they modified the corrective actions to only one infraction, to which I disagreed.

My manager informed me of other things that were brought up during my absence that created doubt. She referenced a complaint my direct report gave against my team leader, stating that he was targeting her; she mentioned comments that were made of me being disrespectful when talking to the group, singling her out in group discussions, and talking to the group as if they were children. As a point of reference, the complainant was a white Millennial female. My team leader and I are both black, while he is a member of Generation X, and I, of course, am a Millennial. I gave a rebuttal to the statements and asked for a specific example. None could be provided.

Later that day, one of my direct reports, a white male belonging to Generation X, told me of things that had occurred the week before while I was out on vacation. He mentioned some people received corrective action and told of other things that sparked an investigation. I was told HR and my managers had been on the floor asking questions of the group about how things were going and getting details of the team leader's and my actions toward the group. I was informed separate interviews were held that did not primarily pertain to me, as the group enjoys working with me, but that some people had issues with others. The issues were referring to the team leader.

I followed up with one manager to address any concerns. He stated he asked the group how I was doing and received positive feedback aside from one person who commented everything is good when they see me. This was corrected by the manager as the comment was based on me being put on medical restrictions over the past couple of weeks, preventing me from being on the manufacturing floor as often. That afternoon, I confronted my manager with my frustration of being investigated while I was on vacation. I also informed her I felt as if I was being targeted and harassed by the HR representative. She commented she had heard others in the past make similar statements and was seeing some behaviors as she manages the group's issues and mine. I asked if I had a chance here or if I should just look for other options. She stated she wanted me to continue to work there but needs to figure out how to address the situation.

Similar events of direct targeting continued for months, and I walked on eggshells, not knowing if or when I would be terminated. My level of frustration had grown high, I had no trust in the management team, and these events were affecting my well-being. I even received a phone call from the HR representative during that time questioning if I had a flyer posted on the board selling Jordan brand sneakers. I informed her I hadn't and was asked if I was sure. If you're thinking like I am, I thought ma'am, I would know whether I had something posted. Either way, I again stated that the flyer was not mine. She asked if I knew to who the flyer belonged, and I informed her I did not.

I went to look at the flyer to see what the concern was and why I was being questioned. The flyer had a phone number with an out-of-state area code listed and was not previously approved by HR for posting. I informed my manager again of being targeted. She told me to just keep doing the right things and just ignore the situation. The following day, I saw the HR representative in passing and politely asked her why she thought to call me and ask about the flyer. She responded she had seen me wear Jordan's in the plant. I corrected her and told her I do not wear Jordan's in here. She then fumbled saying that she knows I like sneakers and because I had a new pair on. I walked away and commented I just wanted to understand why she came to me.

I found out later a black male Millennial was also questioned about the flyer and was informed there would be corrective actions that would affect his position. He denied being responsible for the flyer as well and informed her who it belonged to. The owner was a white male Millennial working in another department in the plant. They contacted the owner and attempted to later apologize, but this wasn't enough. I pushed for actions to be taken as had been threatened, but it was unclear if the owner of the flyer received any corrective actions. If nothing else, this was the end of something new.

Chapter 6

Mustard Seed

After deciding to leave that employer, I needed to figure out what was next. I was stepping out on faith the size of a mustard seed, with no plan in place. All I knew was that my chapter there had ended, and I needed something that would not set out to destroy me in many aspects. If you have Baby Boomer parents, you know their perspectives went along the lines of not leaving one job until you have found another. I would normally agree, but it took a lot of constraints to not react in a manner that would negatively reflect my character if I had stayed.

The next day after resigning, I sat in my garage and just looked out into the world, or my small view of it anyway, that resided immediately in front of my home. I sat and listened to the calmness of nature and was left with my thoughts and a composition notebook. The art of writing down and capturing thoughts had seemed to dwindle. There's always value in writing things down and being able to go back and reflect upon what you once thought in a certain moment. I wrote down potential business ventures and other thoughts I could manifest in finding my purpose. The gears in my mind just turn, which can be a gift and a curse. Some random thoughts are hysterical to me, while there are some I must write and capture, so I don't forget. There's a chance it could make sense somewhere down the line.

I believe finding your purpose is not just a solid-state, but fluid and according to the season or moment. Your purpose will be different things to yourself and others, while possibly altering by the time the task is complete. Sometimes I must remind myself to just enjoy the moment and breathe for a while, but the other part of me is always on go. I just don't sit down well.

After reflecting, I took a drive to Orangeburg to look for buildings for a probable business opportunity, but stopped at my hairstylist before I did anything. In the black community, particularly for females, there is an unwritten code that your hairstylist is a safe space. She had heard me express frustrations with that job and felt like I was supposed to do something else. It was pure relief to let her know I left my job, but was unsure of what was next. There was no judgment as she seemed to feel the excitement radiating from me and exuded the same energy back.

When I left there, I looked at locations and stopped by the future location of my family's liquor store. My cousin, who is like my brother, and my uncle, were opening a store around the corner from our family's neighborhood, Sunnyside. I had time since I was job seeking and lent my assistance. I was still helping coach girls' basketball, but it was not enough to occupy my day. Once the store opened, I managed the day-to-day operations, and eventually became an owner once my uncle sold his share. This was nothing I could've imagined, but it kept me busy while I figured out my plan.

One day, while working at the store, I gazed outside the window at a vacant property located across the street. The gears in my head turned once again, and I saw an opportunity in an abandoned

space. I excitedly told my cousin, who was now my business partner, and he could see my vision. The family says we both act alike,
but it's amazing when someone sees your vision and can reciprocate
your vibe all from looking through the lens of a rough canvas.

There are parts of Orangeburg that need a facelift, as there are
buried gems in the town. This was also perfect timing for us as they
were revitalizing the downtown area and we could benefit from the
city revamping the physical appearance of the landscape and side-
walks. Of course, this was all a dream until we could make it come
to fruition. We didn't know who the owner of the vacant building
was and would have to do some digging.

The timing worked out for a reason, as I saw a woman and
her son pull up to this vacant property one day while working at
the store. I was friendly as we exchanged pleasantries from across
the street. My goal was not to make them uneasy but to show my
true interest in the area and see what information they could provide. She was a well-dressed and business-oriented white woman. I
live for joggers and a t-shirt or hoodie for pure comfort, so I tried
my best not to make her nervous, not knowing any preconceived
notions she might have had.

She was welcoming, and I explained who I was and our interest in the property. This initial conversation went well, and she
explained the history behind the property and her family's ties to
Orangeburg. After that, we exchanged information and eventually
entered into a rental agreement to see how this venture would go.
She also had to work out some things with the family regarding the
property, such as probate, so this was perfect.

We conceptualized and made a walk-up convenience store a
reality. There was a smaller building and a larger one behind it,
but our short-term plan was for the smaller building. We had seen

walk-up locations work in places, such as New York, and wanted to do so in Orangeburg to expand our entrepreneurial journey.

This was a family venture getting aspects of this new location to work, and I picked up a lot from my father and others as this work commenced. Once my father sent me down the path of some of the work, I would stay to finish on my own. My dad loves to say he is a jack of all trades and master at none. Well, I try to pick up some of these trades from him. He also likes to say you either have time or money. Since I'm not rich and had left my full-time job, I had more time than anything.

We eventually opened the convenience store, and a car wash was later opened in the space next to the smaller building. Our ambitions were in full throttle. We even had the Mayor of Orangeburg stop by to congratulate us. He mentioned he heard what we were doing and saw us doing things in the area and wanted to express this to us. Owning a business, or businesses, is nowhere an easy feat, but it is worth it. It is worth it, even more, when others recognize your efforts. Not to mention, we bought the property after our rental agreement ended. We now owned two commercial properties in the town that raised us.

Momentum was building from an entrepreneurial sense, but I was still without full-time employment. Healthcare is also expensive in the private sector. They based my rates on what I made the previous year with my employer, although I explained I was no longer working there and making nowhere near the money I once was. At that point, it was clear I needed to look back at entering the workforce.

I wasn't sure I wanted to go back into the manufacturing industry, but wanted to keep my options open. One of my mentors from my first employer was doing some work as a consultant and traveling the world. I wasn't sure if this was what I wanted to do, seeing as how my experience in Washington turned out; however, this was an excellent opportunity to see the world, and I didn't say no. I also was asked about managing the program I had been hired into out of college. This would allow me to do recruiting and continue to mold the young lives of engineers entering the workforce. The only catch would be that I would have to move to Memphis, Tennessee. Everything was going well in South Carolina, and I was not interested in moving. Finally, an opportunity came with a large employer that differed from what I had been doing.

I started back working full-time, with benefits, and thought God's timing is impeccable! Orientation was amazing, and I met some great people. I even loved the tenets the company promoted. There was also a very diverse company makeup, so all seemed promising. When I got to my assigned location, it was not the sunflower and roses as I had thought. I would work the night shift, which was a benefit as most of the big decision-makers were only there during the day. This also allowed me to coach and maintain the store during the day, though there was minimum time for sleep. A wise friend from college once told me you'll sleep when you're dead. She's a doctor in the medical field, so I think there's some truth to that.

I worked at this place but knew this wasn't where I saw my long-term career. There were some mental aspects of this job I would endure, but a lot of physical aspects as well that would accompany. I knew I was there to gain something from this experience and was open to receiving what God was trying to do in that season.

There were plenty of times I functioned while sleep-deprived and physically tired. I worked off to the side or walked the floor often, saying, "Lord, I get it." In every experience, there is a lesson. I had stepped out on faith and had calmed down from when I was with my previous employer, but still knew there was more for me to learn. I recited other mantras and had several talks with Jesus, only to realize I had to learn yet another lesson in patience.

Patience was never my strong suit, but was a part of my faith walk. He bailed me out when I needed to return to work, as I had spent most of what I had saved up, but did I truly understand the lesson of patience with Him coming through when I needed him and according to His timing? The quick answer was no; hence, the experience with my new employer.

The environment physically wore me down and I needed to have knee surgery. I had gone through pills, creams, and cortisone shots like it were nothing; yet I was experiencing swelling and pain every time I went to work. I went out for surgery and rushed to get back. Based on what I previously said, my sentiments were, I wasn't sure why. After returning, it was solidified that I needed to find something else to continue my career growth.

I began applying for jobs every time I heard someone mention a location was hiring. I was open to the manufacturing industry once again, but tried to remain patient as I waited for God to place me where He wanted me to be. In the interim, my other knee gave me issues and was found to be in much worse shape than the one I had already had surgery on. The pain was only mitigated because something close to the cortisone the doctor tried had lessened what I was feeling.

While waiting to schedule surgery, I had an unfortunate encounter with a manager on the floor in front of associates. He came out of the office to berate and belittle me in front of others. God had worked on me but was not done with me. My people are in place for the shift to begin. I walked around and breathed, but it was not calming me fast enough. I then walked to my car and sat in it, letting out my frustrations. If anyone saw me, I'm sure I looked insane. I called my sister and told her I was over it, and she merely asked could I resign and financially sustain myself like I had the last time. Hmm… a valid point, as I had not built my savings up to where I would have liked.

I gathered myself and went back inside. I couldn't let the situation ride and went to find my manager. He was a tall and heavy-set black man who towered over me. I was going to let go of what had torn me up since I had last seen him about an hour earlier. When I saw him, I told him I needed a minute of his time. This conversation was going to be risky, but I was going to let it ride. I informed my manager that I was a woman first and that he should never feel that comfortable talking down to me and disrespecting me in that manner again. His look was shocked, but he didn't give a rebuttal. It was business only after that, with him attempting to apologize. My concern for his apology was minimal as I was gearing up to go out again for surgery.

A couple of days before my surgery date, I received a phone call for an in-person interview. I had previously done some phone screens, with one of them leading to an interview. The only issue that existed was the interview was scheduled for the day after my surgery. I had no choice but to inform the recruiter, who said he would get back to me. I doubted they wanted me to come in with crutches, but at that point, I was willing to take that chance if they were. My pain tolerance has always been high, so I gave no thought to the need to take pills or anything to alleviate pain.

The recruiter called me back and asked if I could be there to interview the next morning. I was scheduled to work an overtime day but informed them I would need to leave by midnight. That night was a disaster, and I also had to wrap up things to prepare for my going out for surgery. Hence, I stayed well past midnight until I had to go to make it to my interview. I made it home with enough time to shower and make it to the location. Not a wink of sleep, but I had been in this place before and learned to function from no sleep.

When I had gone on interviews before and had crazy things happen, I usually got the job. Before one interview, my keys fell in the toilet, and I had no sleep the night before either. I finished that interview with barely enough time to make it to a game I was helping to coach that night. There were people assigned to pick me up from the airport. I went to hang out with my line sister and her family and realized there was a concern for my whereabouts well after the fact. The last experience I'll describe was being hit while returning a rental car after an interview. My hopes were high. If someone paid me to recall my responses that day, I couldn't because I was delirious by the time I left.

I had lunch at the location and left to go to basketball practice. Not to mention, I had to get prepared for surgery the next morning. While I was out for surgery, the only call I got from my employer was to ask when I was returning because of the notable increase in orders for the holiday season. In my mind, I was thinking thanks for checking on me…full of sarcasm, of course. I told my family of this insensitive call from my employer, and they asked if I had heard from my interview before the surgery. I had completely forgotten about the interview and figured they had moved on since I didn't hear back.

A couple of weeks before I was gearing up to return to work, I received a phone call from the company I interviewed with before my surgery. They wanted to extend an offer but had waited as they knew I needed to recover from my surgery. They also asked how my surgery went and if I was better. I felt like this was genuine concern, none that I had experienced with my current employer. The decision was simply to leave based on this. I knew where I was didn't appear to be where I needed to be. It only took two knee surgeries, with screws in both knees, for me to solidify this. God's timing is perfect!

Chapter 7

Growth but Still Growing

It seemed like the next opportunity was promising. This company was willing to wait for me to recover from surgery, so they must have wanted to hire me. This minor act shows the importance they placed on people and compelled my desire to become a part of this organization. The orientation period was enlightening and acclimated me to the company. My new manager came to look for me while I was in orientation and wanted to ensure I had the things I needed to get started. He was a white male member of the Baby Boomer generation and exemplified traits of humility, business savviness, transparency, and, most importantly, compassion. There were no physical differences seen when we worked together as I sensed his genuineness to help me grow, and he became a mentor, which he still is to this day.

I went to the area where I would work in a training capacity. The physical makeup of the team was very similar to those of other manufacturing organizations in which I had worked. There were primarily white males belonging to Generation X, with some Baby

Boomers and Millennials sprinkled in. I wanted to learn the process and be transparent about who I am, with the team with whom I was working. From the start, I built a rapport with an unlikely ally. We came from different walks of life, demographically, but our stories were very similar. He would grow to be a good friend and helpful as I navigated this new company.

I was training with another supervisor but realized some opportunities within the team. Regardless, I was merely training and needed to learn more about the company and how it functions while in my new role. Sometimes the person I was training with was out, and I was left to work with the team independently. I took this time to also build camaraderie with other supervisors, with whom I found a mentor in one of them. While I was training, I learned more about how the team worked. I scheduled a meeting with the manager of the area, his supervisors, and the person who was training me. This meeting would present how one process would work to elevate the needs of the technical team. There seemed to be a mutual alignment from this, and we were moving forward.

While training out of town, I met with the site's Technical Manager, the supervisor who was mentoring me, and another trainee to be a Technical Manager for a place in the future. I was asked to take over the area I was training as they coordinated other moves in the plant. I agreed to take over the team and was excited about the opportunity ahead. At that moment, I was pulled from training to return to the team as the plan was being announced.

The Technical Manager for the site came to the meeting with my team. I was now solely managing the next day and asked how I was going to achieve the required certifications for the group within the year. Stunned by the initial push as I tried to get things in line, I was open and excited about the challenge. The team was competent, and it was my goal to show everyone else they could do it. They were undoubtedly talented people who would be needed to make things happen.

One person was out on medical leave during the announcement. The supervisor I was training with was working to move him out of the group. He blatantly told me he wouldn't work well for me, and I should let the move occur as he would probably have a problem working for a black female. Excuse me, sir, what?! He tried to explain because of how he was and his background, and I told him I would see for myself. I had heard good things about this person, alongside some opportunities. However, I'm a person not easily tainted by what is heard. I like to form opinions for myself. When the person returned from leave, we had an open and honest conversation and had a great working relationship.

The team improved as I learned more about the process and sought to work with them to also educate myself. My time was balanced between the aspects of my job and working with my peers in production. We gained traction and performed better to achieve the certification goals that were questioned when taking over the team.

While things were going well at work, I eventually gave up coaching at my high school alma mater once my niece completed her basketball season and graduated. My time coaching was nothing I took for granted, and I am proud to say I have mentored young ladies who have gone off to college receiving Ph.D.'s, are doctoral candidates, professional basketball players, coaches, and numerous other professional titles. While I am proud of their titles,

I am euphoric in knowing they urge and shape other minds in the process. I've heard my conversations come full circle in some discussions with the shock factor that they were listening and not simply just hearing me speak. Then they remind me, "Yes, Coach. We were listening."

As I mentioned, I don't enjoy being stagnant and picking up another endeavor. I am passionate about DIY projects that usually get me hurt, but I love doing them. However, I still desired more and pursued higher educational goals. My doctorate was up next but would be a challenge with working full-time. I discussed this with my manager, who was fully supportive. Below is what I described as my rationale for enrolling.

Throughout my life, I was taught that education is a crucial component of development today. The need for lifelong learning is an essential aspect of one's development. The industry is rapidly changing and demanding a better understanding of financial analysis and contingency planning. With the economic environment playing a pivotal role in the industrial society, it is beneficial to have both the technical background and the conceptual skills required to operate the business with the awareness of the incurring cost involved, including human capital. This requires an individual to develop many lifelong-learning skills. I would like to continue my education by pursuing my Doctoral Degree in Business Administration (DBA) with a concentration in Leadership. My reasoning for this is so I may learn various techniques and experiences from the classroom and apply them to a professional environment. After gaining this relevant and extensive experience, I plan to use a combination of my experiences, education, and motivation to excel as a path to advancement within my company. Thus, allowing me the tools needed to excel in the competitive workplace by making myself well-rounded in the functioning worlds of business, technology, and manufacturing. With the ever-changing pace of management driven by employee engagement and empowerment, it is essential to obtain the credentials to create and implement sustainable progress. Therefore, receiving another level of education can only expand my development.

I feel that additional preparation in management obtained through graduate study would be needed to achieve my goal. I have many enduring experiences that would prepare me for the arduous nature of a doctoral program. This is proven by excelling in my undergraduate and graduate degree programs and completing both with honors. I joined and participated in several organizations that provided networking opportunities, worked collectively on projects, and developed leadership and other essential skills needed for success in my career, graduate studies, and life. I exemplified this through my service as the Assistant to the Programs Director for the College of Engineering at North Carolina A&T State University. During this time, I was exposed to many managerial tasks, including acting as the liaison between the University and company representatives in implementing new educational standards put forth by the Dean of the College of Engineering, constructing an innovative Marketing Brochure and Newsletter, editing a Senior Design Manual for the members and companies of the Engineering Advisory Board so that the student's work would be illustrated to its contributors. Professionally, I have been a part of several initiatives that promote diversity for both minorities and women.

An example of this would be my involvement in a women's forum. At this forum, I was a panelist focusing on generational diversity and women's roles in the workplace, specifically in the manufacturing environment. Pursuing this degree delves into my desire to emphasize and promote minorities and women in the workplace. Most companies have started an initiative to encourage minorities into business roles, as it directly correlates with the likeness of management and their respective consumers. I would like my involvement to focus on leading these drive-through affinity groups, emphasizing employee engagement.

My professional experiences have allotted me opportunities to exhibit my managerial capabilities through roles and tasks of increasing responsibility. They include being certified to manage contractors' work while on the premises, facilitating surveys to reduce cost and increase savings, managing essential projects, and implementing and evaluating programs to remain following company and OSHA standards. I have recently focused on structuring team development and engagement while achieving sustainable results. While new to the role, my team was challenged to obtain certifications concentrating on standardization and results-driven progress. Initially, there were no metrics to indicate how the area was trending monthly, and the indicators were not driving results. To get the team involved, I discussed the site's needs and opportunities for improvement. I empowered them to be owners of their processes. Through this effort, we could grasp which areas should be focused on more closely to continue to drive improvement. Thus, leading to decreased downtime for the site that has been sustained for over a year. Their engagement in a structured process contributed to the team earning the certification focused on progress driven by results. The standardization certification directly aligns with decreased downtime and increased productivity. Members of the group could not locate the parts and tools needed to properly perform their tasks. By standardizing the area and maintaining results, the team obtained the standardization certification, which was achieved within one year. Overall, this process required commitment from the group, planning, scheduling of tasks, and logistics to properly execute these actions while keeping the area running efficiently.

I have many characteristics essential for performing well in graduate school. These include honesty, integrity, drive, initiative, and the willingness to take on increasingly challenging and demanding tasks. Also, I am very educated and have tremendous reasoning skills combined with business acumen, technical aptitude, interpersonal savvy, and the ability to learn on the fly. This exhibits a balance of self-motivation, desire for success, and passion for working with others. Aside from my professional attributes and contributions, I have utilized my skillset in mentoring and being an Assistant Coach for Orangeburg Wilkinson High School Girls Basketball Team. My focus is on developing successful student-athletes, emphasizing being a student foremost. I aid in developing these young ladies academically and instill in them the characteristics and skills that they will need to navigate through life.

These lessons are implemented in a team setting. They can work together toward a common goal, understand strategic thinking, and govern themselves through quick response situations developed in scenario-based training. These are essential characteristics developed through both professional and personal experiences. I have an openness and willingness to share with others. My analytical skills and intellectual curiosity will allow me to handle these situations and become successful in a rigorous academic program while later developing others and processes.

This was built upon foundational facets of my grandparents' stressing the importance of education and family support. Also, my best friend, who is like my sister, and the many opportunities professional opportunities have afforded me. This was my obligation to do more and make a change. While this would not be a medical degree, I would be the first doctor in my family, and wanted to ensure the younger generations saw the significance of doing so. An excerpt from the dedication in my dissertation is listed below.

This study is dedicated to my family, my ancestors, and the lineage thereafter. I hope we continue to blaze trails and be an example for those to come. This is important in changing the narrative and declaring a new standard. In the words of Ralph Waldo Emerson, "Do not go where the path may lead, go instead where there is no path and leave a trail."

On March 27, 2018, as I was driving to work, there seemed to be things going on with me personally and professionally. I couldn't put my finger on what I was feeling, but looking back, it was anxiety. Why was I anxious? How could I get control of this? Then, as I traveled south on I-77, there were rocks on the road falling from a truck up ahead. They were hitting my car and possibly causing damage. To create some distance and safely get past the debris, I applied my brakes, but instead of stopping, my car slid across the lanes. I couldn't control the vehicle and saw the concrete wall for an overpass. I was preparing to brace myself for the hit and flip over. Whatever was to come was to come. I couldn't fight or get control any longer. Suddenly, the car slowed down. The back end of the vehicle tapped the concrete wall and eventually lined me back out, allowing the car to come to a complete stop.

After realizing I was still alive and had injured no one, I cried hysterically. I tried to calm myself down but couldn't. I called my sister, but she couldn't provide comfort to me. I called my dad, who provided some comfort and prayed with me, but it wasn't enough.

I went into work broken and confused. One of my good friends at work came outside, where I was crying hysterically again, and just sat with me. I gathered myself to finish the day, but I was not of much value.

I realized my help wasn't supposed to be in the phone calls I made, but on God, who had saved me and provided what I needed. The realization that it was him whom I needed to seek. After, one of my line sisters posted a scripture on Facebook that was fitting for that moment. Psalm 143: 8-12 (NIV) reads, "Let the morning bring me word of your unfailing love, for I have put my trust in you. Show me the way I should go, for to you I entrust my life. Rescue me from my enemies, LORD, for I hide myself in you. Teach me to do your will, for you are my God; may your good Spirit lead me on level ground. For your name's sake, LORD, preserve my life; in your righteousness, bring me out of trouble. In your unfailing love, silence my enemies; destroy all my foes, for I am your servant." That moment was to seek Him and not others in my time of need. I was admitted to Liberty University for my doctoral program. Liberty is a Christian school rooted in biblical foundations. I was unsure how this would work out as my doctorate was supposed to be on my practical professional experiences. Reflecting on that day made it abundantly clear why I was enrolling in this school. There was something more I still needed to keep me balanced.

As aforementioned, I worked on my doctorate as I continued to work. This was no easy feat, but capable through the support of those around me. Professionally, there was my mentor and now former manager, my direct reports, and another supervisor who pushed me when I felt like I had enough.

While working on an ongoing issue at work one evening, tensions ran high between the new Area Manager and me. I was fully invested in my team and took it personally when their efforts were criticized. I lost my cool and told the team we would reconvene the next day. A lot was going on for me, but I was more so upset with myself that I had let someone take me out of my element. This is what I had worked so hard on during my time away and grown to get away from. I was even more upset that my team had seen this. I was not a pushover but focused on getting my point across, being direct, and minimizing emotion. The past has taught me some things, so I ensured to practice this while working on myself. I apologized to my team the next day, but they fully supported me. We worked to resolve the issue soon afterward and went on business as usual.

As management roles changed, I adjusted to new people and expectations. A new manager in the area could have been more knowledgeable and helpful. However, that was not the case. For my new direct manager, I was clashing some due to what the new Area Manager was conveying to him. I sought insight from my mentor to address, as he had worked through management adjustments much better than I had in the past.

One day, my new manager asked me what I thought about doing his job. I told him I hadn't, and we had further discussion as to what drove my thoughts. There were periods when I felt I needed to be an individual contributor again, as life could be much easier. However, I thought I was meant for something more than just me.

During our discussion, I mentioned I needed to get through six months or more to get past a load of classes. The next thing I knew, he was on to his next move, and his position was posted. The timeline was much faster than I thought, and I was awarded his job and in place within a couple of months. A new job and juggling more classes than I had before. As the saying goes, "You want to tell God a joke; tell him your plans

Chapter 8
I Am Enough

I moved into a new role of managing my former peers. Moving to this role was shocking to some because my name wasn't in the conversation of people considered amongst the rumor mills. I realized conversations were being had about me, and people were checking LinkedIn to understand my background. I started to jokingly get a t-shirt with my resume made onto it or randomly place copies of my resume out there for those intrigued. I was a mystery to some, and others pondered how I had surpassed others who had been there for several years. My approach has always been to let the work speak for me thus, there was no need to yell at the top of my lungs that the team I had been leading had made a significant turnaround in the plant.

It's never a peaceful transition as you lead your former peers. Still, I felt it was necessary to have a conversation with those interested in my current job. It was essential to let them know my expectations of having their full support. Plus, to determine how I could best provide exposure for them as potential backfills if I left the position.

This was a new opportunity for me. In this role, I needed to replicate the actions of becoming a team throughout the plant.

My manager was the Operations Manager. We sought to work together to bridge the gap of a finger-pointing culture between production and maintenance. My manager was an excellent people's leader and allowed me autonomy while allowing me to myself. He was a white male belonging to Generation X, but he got me. Not to mention I was now working alongside my mentor, and first manager, as a peer. They both guided me and poured into my development, along with others.

I could make this seem like a fairytale and say everyone got along with my team making tremendous strides, but this isn't a fictional depiction of events. Some people were not happy with my being in the role and wanted out. I stopped nothing that would retain them and align with their future endeavors should opportunities present themselves for them. With that, I had to look for and identify others that would be influential in leadership roles. While building the team, we worked on some of the historically more complex areas regarding production and reliability. Through improving performance, we formed cross-functional teams and peeled back the proverbial onion. Through this teamwork, we were making traction. Then, as most experienced, here comes management during COVID-19.

COVID-19 brought about management during unprecedented times. I had no problem with managing through organizational agility and aligning the team as needed, but this proved to be a fresh challenge for all. This led to reduced production and the need to still meet cost objectives. Some people were furloughed and opted not to work while we reduced productivity. Our norm became temperature checks, extra cleaning, and staggering work to not risk anyone's safety. You were considered 'Patient Zero' if you contracted it at that time. Currently, it seems as if most people you know have had it, and for those who haven't, most have had symptoms and not been tested.

This changed the perception of work. Most people learned they could survive being an entrepreneur or that it was too risky to return to the workplace. This truly impacted the workforce and competencies of management, technicians, operators, and all other integral functions of an organization at discrete sites. After dealing with it for over a year and other influences, my manager and HR manager left the company. I had developed a friendship and rapport with them both and was sad to see them leave. Soon after, my mentor announced he was going to retire. We had worked well together. Afterward, I realized he had been developing and preparing me for this all along based on him involving me in several things. We split technical duties for the plant, and I would miss our balance.

Because of my mentor's retirement announcement, the site realigned the technical management structure. I assumed responsibility overall for the technical group. This was happening during the impact of COVID, my mentor being out for surgery before retiring, a new manager, and trying to finish school. To say my stress level was high is an understatement! I was forming a new team but had some people resign, which complicated things further. I planned to align the unit where their experience and competencies best fit it. There were multiple scenarios developed, as management has taught me to be innovative and have contingency plans A through Z in place. You sometimes must double up on the alphabet with plan AA (no pun intended).

With the changes, I now reported to the Plant Manager, who was a tough female Baby Boomer with lots of experience in the industry.

The thing with new managers is getting acclimated. Although I had worked with her before, it was never in a direct reporting structure as we currently had. She challenged me and taught me to cover all aspects and worked to develop me, allowing me the opportunities I deserved. She had knocked down many barriers to being a female in the industry. As a result, there were some gems to pick up. With any change, I would be unauthentically me if I told you we sang Kumbaya and chanted positive affirmations. However, this builds people when others challenge them. We had to work on communicating with one another about what works and find our common ground. She pushed me and saw more in me than I frankly saw in myself or wanted to see. I was perfectly content staying in the realm where I had worked and had built together with the team. Not to mention, the people were continuing to evolve, and I am proud that many of them were promoted into salaried roles. They trusted me being new and worked with me; it was only fair that I reached back and gave them an opportunity.

The new organization was in place, but we knew the skillsets were lost in people, leaving either through attrition or unplanned departures. I also could free up some time as I finally finished my doctoral program and was now Dr. Janelle A. Jordan, DBA. My dissertation focused on Generational Communication Disparities in Leadership, and this was something I took to heart even more than before. I planned to do what I explained in my rationale for obtaining my degree and implementing my workplace learnings.

With this new team, we would need to work on building the foundations of the team once again, inclusive of the new leaders that were in place. It was not easy, but the leaders needed to get the required training, and I was accessible to help lead them to transfer this guidance to the team. It was also a learning opportunity as I realized I made assumptions that these new leaders knew what I knew, especially if they were promoted internally. All assumptions had to be thrown out the window, and there was work to be done not solely by me, but through leveraging the strengths of others on the team. We were developing plans and making slow progress, then boom! The Plant Manager was retiring. This would be another change in guidance and expectations provided as I once again had adjusted to my new manager.

As new management entered, there was a get-to-know-you period once again. I'd done well with my time there and was listed as having high potential within the company. I wanted to maintain this stance with the proper support. Yet, here was a person who was unfamiliar with me, and we had to work together to balance expectations while driving progress. He was a white male and a member of Generation X. I had heard things before his arrival, but I was consistent in forming my opinion.

Upon our initial meeting, I could tell he was slightly thrown off. Regardless of people wearing masks, I read the eyes and body language. Nonverbal communication was a part of my dissertation, so I keened in on the cues. I took him being thrown off was because of my physical appearance, mainly my hair. My hair was straightened in my profile's professional picture, and I wore a button-down shirt. However, in person, I had crotched faux locks in my hair. Let's be clear, my hair is natural, and I live in the South, where it is always hot and humid much of the year. It was either wear protective styles or leave with an afro daily. I mentioned I change my hair often, and we moved past this.

He covered his academic, professional, and personal background, and I followed with the same. When I spoke of my academic background, he mentioned he hadn't met too many people with more education than him. I found this to be funny as I knew many people with doctoral degrees but fought the urge to ask about the implied meaning. I took note but felt this might be a problem from a narcissistic standpoint, not being my own. There is always a honeymoon phase with new people in place. There seemed to be a good start, but things took on a distinct feeling as time went on. I was feeling like I was in a losing battle and did not have the proper support.

It was mentioned that the team needed to reach out to our new manager if we thought about doing something else and potentially thought about leaving. I met with my manager to address my frustration and potential intent to look elsewhere. We had spoken of a viable career path in HR previously, but it would be a couple of years out. My purpose in going to talk to him was to express incongruences and ask for help. Not to mention, I was to fill two roles as I moved someone out of their position. They had some opportunities to develop and lacked in fulfilling their responsibility, so I picked up some of the slack, anyway. I was told in not so many words I did a lot for my team and needed to address the issue with this person. Otherwise, it would reflect on me. I gave this person an option, which was more respectful to what was suggested by my manager. They took the offer, but I would be left with my job and theirs, as the position was vacant.

I listed the rationale for discussion with my manager as being on the team, but not included. My team's decisions were discussed without my involvement. I was a dumping ground, lacking HR support from multiple aspects where they've lapsed in responsibility for action, follow-up from management outside of the site, and lack of resources to achieve progress. Not to mention, we struggled to be competitive in pay. Actions needed in my group were enormous, and the ability to execute with knowledgeable personnel leaving presented a complex challenge. This also limited my time to take a vacation, which had more discussion than needed to sell time back or lose it from HR. I did not feel the support to fulfill this role was adequate. My manager asked what would alleviate this frustration? Our discussion was based on moving into the HR function and him seeing what opportunities would be available.

He would assist with some actions to free up my time. We would circle back in a couple of weeks to gauge how I felt and my thoughts. Also, discussions of going external to the site to obtain people from his previous location had sparked issues and concerns within my team. A couple of others had already joined from his last location, leading to anxieties about plans to replace people already in position. He assured me he had not done so, but later found out one person he brought along had.

With a plan for help in place, I received a message that some people in HR would reach out for contact discussions. This would help me see where my interest could reside in the future. When we informally met for me to receive performance shares, we briefly discussed our conversation regarding HR and his making contacts for it to move quickly. I informed him I was not looking for a change in roles immediately. I conveyed my family dynamic because of the passing of my stepmother and tried to assist and be available to my father. He mentioned he didn't know it was a factor, although we discussed it in our initial meeting, and he noted it. We covered the vacant position on the team, which I was not informed was being reopened. The position was reopened when I was out on vacation to accommodate someone the HR Manager was familiar with from his previous location. It is imperative to note the lack of trust with the HR Manager. He sought opportunities to direct negative attention to my team as he used to do my role at another plant. My manager said it could be ideal for us to switch positions, but he didn't think the HR Manager could do my job.

Later, I reviewed my training plan for the role and development plan with my manager. Part of the discussion was surrounding details in which he mentioned I should be more vocal and address things more quickly instead of waiting until the fourth time and going 0 to 100 when responding. Due to time constraints and going to prepare for another meeting, I held the rebuttal off until the appropriate time. I discussed with some HR representatives regarding backgrounds and facets of the HR function. This was an information-sharing meeting where I gained additional knowledge of potential roles and progression.

I had a meeting with the new Operations Manager, who my manager had brought along from his previous site. She was a white female and a member of Generation X… I could sense some alpha female traits and felt this would be an intriguing mix. In my previous experience, I witnessed two females be caddy with one another, and I did not want that depiction. We discussed her perception of mounting tensions and wished to ensure alignment in the team and in front of others since we were peers. She explained we started at a good place but felt our relationship was declining. She felt hostility and did not want me to be angry.

She stated she knew I had a lot going on. I explained I could be direct and merely gave rebuttals to her statements. I was not angry as it was no reason to be, as being angry required too much energy. She asked that we stand united in front of the team and that I did not address her in the meeting as her team would think it was alright to do so. We spoke about things outside of the meeting. I agreed with her and asked for the same in return, as my statement was only in response to her comment and had no ill-intent. This led me to rethink the derailer discussion that was brought up with my manager. This was like comments our HR Manager made to our manager that he had made me mad during an exchange. Was a characterization building against me? Was I being labeled the angry black woman I fought so hard not to be?

I continued with my work, but felt something else was brewing beneath the surface. Nothing had seemed to change from the conversation with my manager, and I still was fighting HR, who appeared to have no interest in supporting me. I emailed the HR Manager to follow up on two unresolved issues and copied our manager on one of the two. The premise was based on a continued lack of support and assistance in resolving identified problems for my team. The HR Manager came to see me the next day about the email and how he addressed it. He asked that I refrain from copying our manager on emails and that we resolve amongst ourselves as peers before involving him. He stated he didn't like it and was upset about it. I said I could comply but asked for the same respect as he had done the same to me as we were discussing things and he had given feedback about me being upset. While not in email, the result still applies.

My focus was now being directed to the new year and being able to form a new team that would help drive progress. I had discussions with others respected in the HR realm and those who had retired. This helped to shape my outlook on how to move forward. I was asked to stop by my manager's office for a pay increase for being deemed a high potential performer. We discussed me talking to other resources, including the one he suggested. I noted I would like to stay in the role while working on HR projects on the side to develop my exposure once the critical vacancy was filled. It would also allow me to see what aspect of HR a good fit would be. He asked what had changed. I told him my additional conversations guided me to my current stance to make a conscious decision on which direction in HR I would like to go. This is besides the upcoming organizational changes I was implementing to address our reliability issues. He replied he would need to reflect on this, as he already had the ball rolling with my replacement planning in place. My manager mentioned reaching out and informing upper management external to the plant of my intent to leave the role. He had approval for me to go into an HR Business Partner position.

Also, he stated how would he know I wouldn't change my mind in six months and feel burned out again. Then he would need to start all over. I told him it was a fair statement and noted in the previous conversation that I am not entirely dismissing a technical role and may want to come back at some point. However, I didn't want to rush to move if it didn't fit my development. My manager said he would need to reflect on it and asked me to do the same and bring back five focus areas that would push progress for my group in the next year as my priorities. We were then to discuss the following day.

We met the following day, and I had the five priorities, but I sensed he would do what he had already planned, anyway. I was going to email the requested list but thought differently about it, as they could help someone taking my role. Hence, I talked through them at our meeting. I told him I had reflected and still think the best plan for me would be to stay in my role and do HR projects on the side. For example, the recruiting plan I had emailed to him and the HR Manager to find my own resources. I told him I felt as if he would do what he felt regardless of what I had thought or prepared. I noted the focus areas for the team, and he then provided his thoughts. He stated his gut was telling him I need to go to HR because he thinks I'll leave if I stay in my role. The options were to work for the current HR Manager as a Business Partner, who I informed him I do not trust as he knows the background of unresolved issues and focused on calling out problems in my group because of his experience rather than helping me. There was a continued lack of support there. He asked, what if the HR Manager was no longer in the role? Would that change my mind? I told him I would need to think about it. The other option would be the same role next door at our sister location, but he would need to talk to someone, and I would need to interview. I told him I would think about it, but did not want to be pushed to someone else.

After he started his stance, I stated I thought the previous weeks intended to work on some getting contacts for me to discuss the HR roles and for him to alleviate some issues on my behalf. While he took items on, not one thing has led to a resolution, and more specifically, there are no more people in the door to assist. As he moved quickly for my succession, I also referenced how moves are workable now with technical resources, and I am still asking and lacking support? I also brought up the derailers he previously mentioned to discuss meetings with others on the team that seemed to contribute to his thoughts on a common theme. The narrative he adopted is based on one-sided feedback. I noted the unconscientious bias both ways, but how am I perceived as angry when comments are made as opposed to being direct? I informed him I was straightforward, but not angry. This is the same approach used to address me, but it stuck with me. I also reminded him when he was called out for being angry based on his comments, and he dismissed it, as that's not even close to angry.

I was not afforded the same leniency. I informed my manager of my critique of being defensive before when given feedback, so there is a balance of listening and commenting. He perceived my 0 to 100 reactions from people on the team who understand the circumstances and were still not helping. If I've addressed comments previously, why would a person feel compelled to mention them multiple times to make it to a fourth time, in gaining my reaction? His help was needed in leveling the playing field.

There was still a lack of follow-up from HR, and I also worked to seek my support and references in the HR field and reflected. I would not gain from the Business Partner role and would like to ensure I am aligned with the potential position instead of being pushed in.

I was told the career path would be for me to go into the Business Partner role, Recruiting, and possibly HR Manager at a small plant. The level would be less than what I was currently at, but I would keep my pay. Otherwise, I need to tell him what path I'm choosing. People were aware of my move up to the Country Director. If you have common sense like me, why would the director know who I am and have an interest in my movement? This was pure amateur manipulation.

I also got People Review feedback, and while there were positive things and opportunities, I was still noted as being 'green' or, in other words, new. I told him I would think about our discussion and get back to him. Before concluding, I told him there is internal experience, but there is also external experience I have. My manager was informed that people have tried to sell me short my entire career. I'm more than that with my experience and education outside of the company. No one has asked me to expound directly about it, and no one can speak better for me than myself. In other words, I was not working to take a lesser role than what I felt I deserved. Others have taken the position to serve as the HR Manager with no experience. Still, those I have accumulated were not sufficient. I was still, seemingly, not enough.

My manager and I met again to discuss my career path. I told him I did not want to rush and that he could proceed with posting my job if he needed to do so, and I would work to find my position. I explained it was not advantageous for me to take on the offered role. He then responded that the HR Manager would not be on the job long and trust him. My response was that I am not privy to the information he has and would like to see things unfold before I would consider applying. He stated he would like to move me to the HR Manager role, but others stated I need to experience HR first and then move into the position. At that point, I realized anything I said at the end of the previous meeting was a waste of my oxygen.

I then pondered and asked if this would be premised on performance or development based on earlier comments regarding pay level. If it was genuinely developmental, why would I lose my status if it's a developmental role while others have kept theirs? The reply differed from what was stated before; I would retain my level since it would be developmental, as I became deemed a high potential employee. My manager said he preferred I move into the role he offered and then post my position because of the questions it would pose and how it would look, instead of just posting my job with no role identified for me. I informed him I was not concerned about the perception of others and did not want to hold up his plan. He asked when I would like to discuss with my team, which would occur after I returned from vacation. I had no intention of committing to anything blindly, and the confidentiality of my manager had been compromised due to comments being made outside of those persons he mentioned were aware of the situation. While talking, he also mentioned the potential of others bidding on my job and named the HR Manager possibly applying. He said I could still think over whether or not I want him to post my position while I'm off and get back to him.

When we met again after my return from vacation, it was to discuss what I would say to my team. I told my manager nothing had changed. I would tell them my position would be posted, and I would look for other opportunities. He stated they will use the message that I have been called to other functions in the group to be communicated later. I told him the message sounded like fluff, and he replied it was since I did not know what I wanted to do. Moreover, he mentioned I would still be on payroll and needed to find a position to get off. He explained further that every person has a role, and I couldn't just have one. I told him I understood the concept.

We met a couple of weeks later to discuss work done during a down period. It seemed as if the conversation was driven unfavorably toward my team's performance. He also discussed his comment on the timeframe and getting off the payroll. In the interim, I conveyed to my career partner during a meeting that I was unaware of the timing I had to find another role. My manager questioned me about the statement, and he wanted to circle back with me. He seemed to do some cleanup. I then got clarification that it would be at least 90 days before he expected my role to be filled and I would have to work on finding something. Otherwise, I would be placed in the offered position if I had nothing by then. As a result, I would not just be off the payroll, and that was the rough time frame per my concern regarding the timing discussed.

There was also an offer to talk to the Plant Manager at the sister site next door about doing my current role at their location. It was unclear how I could do my job at another location, but not where I currently was. I then recalled a statement that my manager made stating that managers come and change the team all the time. However, I think it would be based on a mutual agreement or reason. However, I realized my fate with the company was uncertain and how this impacted me. This was especially so after the HR Manager was awarded my job after it was posted. Yes, the same one that did nothing to help and did some other actions during this time, knowing he was going for my role. I wish them all well as I continue to work to pursue my purpose.

Chapter 9

Leadership in Cliche DE&I Organizations

L eadership seems to be the focus of many organizations today, as the historical structure of management has tainted employees' views. Hence, the term leadership will only be used for the rest of this book. Leaders lead people in getting things accomplished, while managers manage processes. We are driven by a world of people focused on titles and diminishing those who are subpar to a certain level, yet everyone should be treated with respect and as equals. It will take leaders to justly implement the initiative of DE&I (Diversity, Equity, and Inclusion) in today's culture.

The DE&I culture is not only dependent on ethnicity, but sexual preferences, gender identification, and other facets, where all demographics are represented in the workplace. Employees' expectations have transcended the outdated practices of the past, leaving employers with the expectations of upholding their company goals surrounding diversity. This is not to be mistaken about filling positions with diverse candidates to merely meet a quota. The hiring of prospective candidates should be based on qualifications, where several minorities have the competencies required to fill positions within organizations. As a minority Millennial, nothing is more disappointing than to think you received a job because of physical attributes. When looking at a blank slate of candidates, it is vital to evaluate everyone equally. Now, I recognize there should be an alignment of personalities within the perspective candidate. However, how do organizations fully drive progress if someone is unwilling to step up and change the rhetoric?

Several considerations should be given to filling roles within organizations. The age and generations in the workforce are significantly different, requiring adjusting to the preferences of younger employees. COVID helped push along the interest of younger generations from several years ago through the advancement of remote work. This period enabled companies to be innovative in carrying out their business practices. Moreover, it didn't hurt, as it helped to mitigate the costs associated with having traditional office locations. Newer generations long from bridging away from the standard work hours and confines of office fronts. Honestly, there is more productivity while working from home, as once becoming engulfed in a task, one can lose a sense of timing. It also allows creativity from the different environments in which a person is exposed. This doesn't even touch on the digital age we live in. People expect things instantly, or even yesterday. This can also be considered the microwave generation.

When considering this new wave of employees, communication preferences are a vital component. There are verbal and nonverbal communication cues that cater to some more than others. These preferences could be categorized generationally, but are built into

the individual and their upbringing. The need for in-person dialogue has transformed. It could dispel some of the preconceived
biases people embody when interacting with those of varying ethnicities. While this is directed towards physical encounters that are
perceived from verbal and nonverbal communication. There is still
a need for human contact to cater to the needs of people.

There is also the need for an appropriate leadership style that
aligns with direct reports. The dictatorial leadership style is no longer applicable today, whether or not you are a minority. There are
aspects of leadership that should be considered that demonstrate
authenticity and relatability. A few leadership styles are servant
leadership, transformational leadership, interpersonal leadership,
empowerment leadership, and emotional leadership. Empowerment leadership and emotional leadership are not what may be
commonly mentioned in forms of literature but are equally essential facets in building an effective team. Each leadership terminol-
ogy mentioned has the intent and meaning implied in the word
proceeding leadership. These models focus on the employee and
driving results with and not through them.

There must be a sense of emotional intelligence in each of these
approaches, used in conjunction with engaged listening. It is vital
that you don't listen to respond but actively take heart to what is
being stated and ensure you properly receive the message. Still, it
must be authentic and transparent. Do not merely make it a part of
your brand in caring about people to attract talent, you must actively
engage in this behavior to identify the root of issues and potential
solutions. Dismiss the thought process of titles and listen to those
who are involved in the process daily. The authority to decide is up
to the leader after hearing an employee out, but it might lead to an
idea never thought about and boost employee morale. Employees,

not just minority Millennials, can gauge an effective leader's genuineness. Someone once mentioned that a manager was trying to be a good person. It instantly made perfect sense to me, and I told them that was the problem. If you are genuinely a good person, you shouldn't have to work hard to be one.

Now that the typical leadership discussions you find in most books are out of the way and can apply to all, regardless of ethnicity. We will get to the meat of leading minorities in the workforce and practices that could be avoided. An essential point of this is noting physical attributes do not make for mutual alignments for leadership. The personality of both parties and the team matter. I've experienced being responsible for leading and mentoring a female as the only female supervisor in the technical ranks. There was no consideration for the hiring needs and mutual fit; it was solely based on gender. If you are paired in a mentor and mentee relationship purely based on physical attributes, find another mentor who can mold and develop you to your potential.

Deliberately work on understanding your blind spots to avoid inherent bias. Our cultural upbringings tremendously influence and shape our outlook on life and our experiences; conversely, it is crucial to understand other sides of the spectrum. If you expect others to give you the benefit of the doubt, be willing to extend that same courtesy to others. Stephen Covey stated, "We judge ourselves by our intentions and others by their behavior." We can't quantitatively measure intentions and track progress as we do actions. Still, we can provide leverage for others in building collateral. People do not expressly set out to do a terrible job. Though we must be open to the thought of giving everyone equal and fair opportunities. It is easy to hold on to the subconscious inclinations of my professional experiences or even those of my family in the events they've witnessed. Yet, we all have a choice to alter how we move forward. This choice is essential in leading minorities in the workforce.

It is also imperative to be mindful of unfittingly identifying a minority as being angry, as doing so is what makes us angry. Because of the prompt desire to have things quickly, the need to be direct and not over-inflate a message resides. For Millennials, we are stuck between Generation X and Generation Z. Thus, we have an appreciation and respect taught to us by our predecessors in the workplace. Still, we understand the fast-paced expectations of our successors. From a black female perspective, most of us have fought hard against the 'angry black woman' stereotype that unfairly gets ascribed to us. We don't all roll our eyes and necks when we talk. Often, the message is the message without the proverbial 'beating around the bush'. We can be direct without being labeled with the adversarial stigma of being angry. We, too, embody passion and character when we talk and appreciate the equality given to the dominant race and gender.

Ultimately, we must create and respect boundaries for one another. Be protective of your personal boundaries and what works for you, but also be mindful of the established limitations of others. While DE&I is a resounding catchphrase in organizations and the need to diversify, understand and embody what it represents and the responsibility of a leader to be a cultural change agent. If you are unwilling to support the stance of the company you represent with this initiative, simply put, GET OFF THE BUS! The world is changing, and there are other opportunities for self-employment or working for companies that have genuinely adopted the approach of being an equal employment opportunity employer. Don't stand in the way of bright minds and the future growth of organizations while being hung up on individualities that differ from your own.

Chapter 10

E. G. O.

This chapter is rooted in the foundations of positive affirmations and guides in being a transparent leader. Ego came up while deciding to leave an employer and was questioned whether or not my ego was getting in the way. The question posed to me made me ponder whether or not having an ego was a bad thing. When we hear the word ego, it is unconsciously affiliated with a negative connotation. It conveys perceptions of narcissism, selfishness, and a sense of pride that should be relinquished. However, I decided this word will not be used destructively and should have an acronym to make it memorable and positive. Ego will be presented as E. G. O., meaning Exuding Greatness Only. This only leads to Expecting Great Opportunities. Yep, you see what I did there. The person you are is all in a mindset and the perception of yourself. So, yes, it's alright to have an E. G. O. and a huge one!

I have found that there is strength in quotes regarding leadership. Yet, it is solely up to the interpreter to apply the message's intent to the individual. These messages are not blanket statements and will not fit every person, group, or situation, but are gems to utilize when needed.

"Managers seek power while leaders seek to empower."

~ Janelle A. Jordan

"We judge ourselves by our intentions and others by their behavior."

~ Stephen Covey

"The struggle you're in today is developing the strength you need tomorrow."

~ Robert Tew

"Success is almost totally dependent upon drive and persistence. The extra energy required to make another effort or try another approach is the secret of winning."

~ Dennis Waitley

"Facts do not change feelings, but feelings change how you perceive facts."

~ Unknown

"It is better to live your sermon than to preach your sermon."

~ Unknown

"If you live for the cheers, you'll die by the boos!"

~ Janese Jordan

"The very best investment you can make is one that "you can't beat," can't be taxed and not even inflation can take away from you. "Ultimately, there's one investment that supersedes all others: Invest in yourself,"

~ Warren Buffett

"Even if you're on the right track, you'll get run over if you just sit there."

~ Will Rogers

"I wanted a perfect ending. Now I've learned, the hard way, that some poems don't rhyme, and some stories don't have a clear beginning, middle, and end. Life is about not knowing, having to change, taking the moment and making the best of it, without knowing what's going to happen next."

~ Gilda Radner

"Short-sighted vision for a long-term dream."

~ Janelle A. Jordan

"We are what we repeatedly do. Excellence, then, is not an act, but a habit."

~ Aristotle

"Live as if you were to die tomorrow. Learn as if you were to live forever."

~ Mahatma Gandhi

"A dream written down with a date becomes a goal. A goal broken down into steps becomes a plan. A plan backed by action makes your dreams come true."

~ Greg Reid

"Be your own walking mission and vision."

~ Janelle A. Jordan

"Leaders cultivate a group of individuals to build an effective team. Managers, on the other hand, are only comfortable with monotonous thinking of individuals."

~ Janelle A. Jordan

"If we're waiting on perfect, we'll be waiting forever." This is a twist heard from, "If we wait until we're ready, we'll be waiting for the rest of our lives."

~ Lemony Snicket

"Remember: Life is short, break the rules (they were made to be broken) Forgive quickly, kiss slowly Love truly, laugh uncontrollably And never regret anything that makes you smile. The clouds are lined with silver and the glass is half full (though the answers won't be found at the bottom) Don't sweat the small stuff, You are who you are meant to be, Dance as if no one's watching, Love as if it's all you know, Dream as if you'll live forever, Live as if you'll die today,"

~ James Dean

While some quotes motivate to exude your E. G. O., some videos are available to promote intrinsic motivation. They may be used individually or within team environments in building effective teams. The links are listed below.

212 The Extra Degree: https://youtu.be/NPEeEqkEjAQ
You Will Not Outwork Me: https://youtu.be/46FPF6pCtY8

This book has permitted me to reflect and hopefully properly convey my experiences, those that are faced by so many minority Millennials in the workforce. As this is not a 'how to' guide for organizational leaders, I hope it enables whoever is reading this content to understand how unconscious biases impact us in conjunction with our cultural upbringing. If nothing else, I hope this book has helped to amend the historical thought processes and opened at least one person's outlook, as they genuinely embody diversity in organizational structures.

This is not only important in the current state but applicable as the demographic is changing and minorities are occupying more of the population. Minorities will eventually play a pivotal part in the makeup of companies and consumers. The time is now to give the recognition and appropriate allotment of positions to those that look like me while being young, black, and educated in Corporate America; simultaneously, the triple threat of being young, black, and female. Whatever the adjective used, the plight of the narrative must change as an opportunity for organizations and not a threat. Often in my career, I wished there was a blueprint and felt the need to create my own. The disparity has been the plight of minority Millennials versus the expectancy of privilege for our counterparts.

About Janelle A. Jordan

Janelle Jordan was born in Bronx, New York, and raised in Orangeburg, South Carolina. She is the daughter of Sandra Jordan and Reverend Andrew (late Shirley) Jordan. Janelle is the youngest of three girls from this union. Her older siblings are Anjelica Jordan-English and Janese Jordan. Janelle is the proud aunt of five nieces and nephews whom she considers her own: Imani Williams, Jamari Williams, Javon Williams, Amaris English, and Arielle English. Also, a brother-in-law, Joel English.

After graduating from Orangeburg Wilkinson High School as an honor student and student-athlete, Janelle was enrolled at North Carolina A & T State University. She graduated Magna Cum Laude with a Bachelor of Science Degree in Electrical Engineering. She later earned her Master of Business Administration Degree in General Management from Troy University and her Doctor of Business Administration Degree in Leadership from Liberty University.

Janelle has over fifteen years of experience, primarily in a corporate manufacturing environment, working in various locations and capacities, with entrepreneurial experience. Most of her professional career has been in the management realm, where she has mentored and developed talent within organizational structures.

Outside of professional experiences, she has served as an Assistant Coach for Varsity Girls' Basketball at Orangeburg Wilkinson High School. While there and beyond, Janelle has mentored several young ladies outside the facets of basketball towards achieving their personal and professional endeavors. Janelle is also a member of Delta Sigma Theta Sorority, Incorporated.

Fresh Ink Group

Independent Multi-media Publisher

Fresh Ink Group / Voice of Indie / GeezWriter / Push Pull Press

ॐ

Hardcovers
Softcovers
All Ebook Formats
Audiobooks
Podcasts
Worldwide Distribution

ॐ

Indie Author Services
Book Development, Editing, Proofing
Graphic/Cover Design
Video/Trailer Production
Website Creation
Social Media Marketing
Writing Contests
Writers' Blogs

ॐ

Authors
Editors
Artists
Experts
Professionals

ॐ

**FreshInkGroup.com
info@FreshInkGroup.com
Twitter: @FreshInkGroup
Facebook.com/FreshInkGroup
LinkedIn: Fresh Ink Group**

Scan to watch the Trailer on YouTube

Scan to order now from Amazon!

A small rural community in the Low Country along Ocean Highway, Green Pond, South Carolina, has long lacked cultural and educational opportunities for its young people's future success. Still, many have gone on to serve in the highest levels of education, government, public service, elected office, business, and medicine. So much success against the odds suggests surely There Must Be Something in the Water. Abbiegail Hugine chronicles the impact just 42 of Green Pond's many children have gone on to make in the world. These inspirational stories prove that, regardless of one's background, we can all find our own paths toward greatness.

*Full-color Interior
8.5-inch Square
Laminate Hardcover
Full-sized Softcover
All Ebook formats*